8/14

SUTTON HOO
The Excavation of a Royal Ship-Burial

SUTTON HOO
THE EXCAVATION OF
A ROYAL SHIP-BURIAL

Charles Green

The Merlin Press
London

First published in 1963
by the *Merlin press Ltd*
3 Manchester Road
London E14 9BD

British Library Cataloguing in Publication Data

Green, Charles
    Sutton Hoo: the excavation of a royal
    ship-burial. — 2nd rev. ed.
    1. Sutton Hoo Ship Burial (England)
    I. Title
    942.6'46   DA155

    ISBN 0-85036-240-7 (hardback)

Figures 8, 9, 21 drawn by Walter Kemsley
Cover designed by Louis Mackay

Typesetting by AKM Associates (UK) Ltd
Ajmal House, Hayes Road, Southall, London
Printed by Adlard & Son Ltd
The Garden City Press
Letchworth, Hertfordshire

Printed in Great Britain

TO IDA

for her patience

CONTENTS

ILLUSTRATIONS

ILLUSTRATIONS

FIGURES IN TEXT

11

PREFACE

T HE REPUBLICATION of this book, revised and, in part, rewritten is a response to a reawakening of public interest in this important site. The years 1975–1983 saw the publication by the British Museum of the results of the pre-war investigations and some post-war excavations on the Anglo-Saxon burial mounds at Sutton Hoo. These four large books (volume III was published in two parts) contain, in great detail, the reports of the excavators and of the specialists who examined the remains of the boat in Barrow No. 1 and the objects recovered from this and other burials. As a result of the most detailed examination in the British Museum laboratories, a number of objects have been newly reconstructed so that their form and suggested function is sometimes very different from that described in the earlier editions of this book. For instance, the stag which was thought to belong to the iron standard has been shown to be part of the sceptre. The form of the helmet has been altered considerably, so that it is now closer to contemporary examples from other sites.

It was thought that a new edition of my father's book, summarising some of the results published in the British Museum volumes would help to spread the scholarship of this great work to a wider readership. But an enormous amount of fascinating information has had to be omitted and anyone keenly interested should consult these four large and lavishly illustrated volumes. Inevitably the publication of these volumes has sparked off a series of reviews and comments in journals published in many parts of Europe.

Another major event which has helped to arouse public interest in the site has been the setting up of a new research project under the control of the Sutton Hoo Research Trust. Work began in 1983. To date, the Research Director, Martin Carver, has carried out a most detailed re-survey of the site. He has excavated areas outside the barrows in an attempt to find the limits of the cemetery, for it is clear that many inhumations, almost certainly of Anglo-Saxon date, were buried at Sutton Hoo adjacent to the barrows. He has studied too the earlier occupation of the site, hardly mentioned in this volume. This is not the place to discuss the work of the new Research Trust, but it is already clear that our ideas of this important site are likely to undergo considerable revision in future years. Anyone interested can keep up to date by subscribing for a small annual sum to the *Bulletin of the Sutton Hoo Research Committee* obtainable from the Sutton Hoo Project Centre, at the University of York. The Sutton Hoo Society Project Centre based at Woodbridge, provides another source of information for those interested in the site.

It was always seen as an essential part of the new research initiative that Sutton Hoo should be placed in its local and regional context. As a result, the Suffolk and Norfolk Archaeological Units have produced plans for a series of detailed fieldwork surveys of parts of the region and a re-examination of the old finds of the period. To date the money could be found only for the survey of the area around Sutton Hoo.

In the twenty five years since the last three chapters on the settlement of East Anglia were written so much new information has come to light and so much work been, and is being, done that to provide a detailed study of the settlement of the region requires a book to itself. The last chapter of this edition is therefore a brief summary of the present state of knowledge and draws heavily on the current research of Chris Scull of Durham University. I am very grateful to him for his assistance.

I am also very grateful to Mrs. R. O'Donoghue for typing the text from an often almost illegible manuscript.

B.G.
Norwich
1986

INTRODUCTION

(To First Edition)

IT IS a commonplace that in the veins of most modern Englishmen there runs the blood of many ancestral peoples. We may turn for example to Daniel Defoe who, in 1703, gave us 'The True-born Englishman', in which he descanted on the mixed descent and summarised it with

> 'The Western Angles all the rest subdued
> A bloody nation, barbarous and rude,
> Who by tenure of the sword possessed
> One part of Britain, and subdued the rest.
> And as great things denominate the small,
> The conquering part gave title to the whole;
> The Scot, Pict, Briton, Roman, Dane, submit,
> And with the English-Saxon all unite.'

And then he goes on to satirise at greater length the Norman strain in the hotch-potch.

But this mongrelism, as it is often called, can be and often is somewhat exaggerated. For Angles, Saxons, Frisians, Jutes, Danes and Norsemen were little more than tribal names of folk of closely-related stocks, of cognate speech and culture. Normans too were transplanted Norsemen somewhat modified by admixture with Saxons and Franks, another northern tribal group. And though the ancient British element, itself compounded of many strains, has modified the 'Nordic' mixture, it has still to be shown that its proportion is considerable in the English amalgam.

Many attempts have been made to prove this: to show, as one writer put it, that in 'those dark and anarchic centuries when, as we conjecture, a certain (probably small) number of North Sea pirates and revolted German mercenaries achieved a measure of political

15

power and perhaps a certain infusion of new blood in the deserted province of Britain. Nay, it actually became a part of English patriotism to prefer this dingy and unattractive origin for our nation to the grandeur of a highly civilized part of the Roman Empire.'

But no competent student of the Dark Ages holds this extreme view. And as modern Dark Age studies progress, the mixed Anglo-Saxon and Scandinavian origin of a large proportion of the English nation becomes ever clearer. It must be noted too that from the first, the settlers commonly called themselves English. Alfred the king, himself a West Saxon, always calls his language 'English' and the peoples of the Heptarchy the 'English-kin', never the 'Saxon-kin'. Oddly at variance with this is the use by the Anglican monks of the name 'Saxons' for the English, but this seems only to be when writing in Latin, in which language earlier writers of the continent had used the name.

Great advances have been made this century in linguistic and historical studies of the Dark Ages. The results of research by physical anthropologists who attempted in the latter part of last century to define the physical types of various strains, fell under suspicion as modern genetic studies revealed the uncertain foundations on which these racial conclusions were erected. But new techniques, in accordance with the greater complexities of their task, are now being devised and practised and in due course should clarify many obscure points. Most significant of all has been the progress in archaeological studies, which for long lagged behind those of the prehistoric and Romano-British periods.

In earlier centuries, remains found in pagan Anglo-Saxon graves were commonly attributed to the Romans. It was not until the latter part of the eighteenth century that the Rev. James Douglas, who excavated a series of Kentish graves, recognised the true origin of his finds. During the nineteenth century many cemeteries were discovered and either excavated or destroyed and from them large quantities of grave-goods came into the hands of museums and private collectors. Still more, particularly the handmade cremation urns, were broken and lost. J. Y. Akerman, Charles Roach Smith and others strove hard to record the best of them, but little attempt was made to study critically this mass of material. And, it must be noted, these earlier evidences were all from graves. It was not until after the Great War of 1914–1918 that the first early Anglo-Saxon dwelling site was recorded.

We owe to three men the great advances in our knowledge which began to be made in the present century. These were Reginald A. Smith of the British Museum, Professor G. Baldwin Brown and, most notable of all, Edward Thurlow Leeds of the Ashmolean Museum, Oxford. They for the first time classified and described this material by comparative methods. The distribution-patterns of the various types of objects were mapped and the sources of these objects were sought, in conjunction with European scholars, in the old Anglo-Saxon homeland. And immediately difficulties began to accrue.

In a famous passage in his *Ecclesiastical History of the English Nation*, Bede (A.D. 672–735), the monk of Jarrow, says: 'Those who came over were of the three most powerful nations in Germany—Saxons, Angles and Jutes. From the Jutes are descended the people of Kent and of the Isle of Wight, and those also in the province of the West Saxons who are to this day called Jutes, seated opposite to the Isle of Wight. From the Saxons, that is the country which is now called Old Saxony, came the East Saxons, the South Saxons and the West Saxons. From the Angles, that is, the country which is called *Angulus*, and which is said, from that time, to remain desert to this day, between the provinces of the Jutes and the Saxons, are descended the East Angles, the Middle Angles, Mercians, all the race of the Northumbrians, that is, of the nations that dwell on the north side of the river Humber, and the other nations of the English.'

With this passage must be considered another by Procopius, a writer of the early sixth century in the Eastern Roman Empire, that Britain was peopled by the Angles, Frisians and Britons. This cannot be summarily dismissed as the mere hearsay of a man living at the the other end of the Roman world for, as will later be seen, it is curiously supported in some ways by the archaeological evidence.

The late H. M. Chadwick in his *Origin of the English Nation* (1907) made the classic analysis of all the evidence given by the earlier authors such as Tacitus, Ptolemy and Orosius, whose works hold references to the North German tribes in the centuries before the Anglo-Saxon migration. From his work and that of later scholars, it seems clear that shortly before the Migration Period began, the continental Saxons inhabited what we now call Holstein, the province between the rivers Eider and Elbe, and East Friesland, the coastal strip of Hanover from the Elbe to the Ems. The Angles were seated to the north of them in what is now Schleswig though, in the century before they came to Britain, many had been moving southward into eastern Holstein, where their characteristic pottery is found side by side with that of Saxon type. The position of the Jutish homeland has occasioned much controversy, but it seems to have lain originally in what is now known as Jutland, the mainland province of Denmark, though many of the Jutes may well have left this province to settle in Saxo-Frisian areas before they came to Britain.

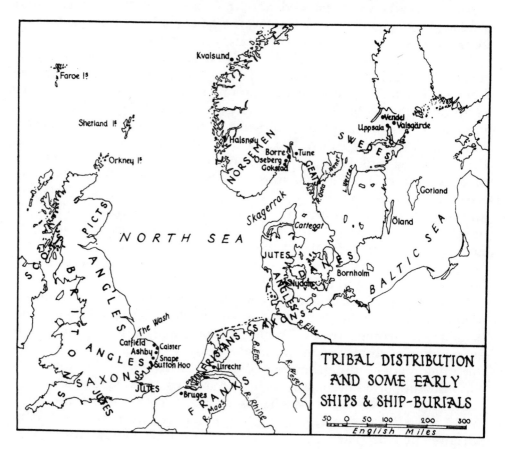

Fig. 1

And this broad distribution seems to be in general accord with the statements of Bede. Other peoples not mentioned by Bede include the Frisians, who occupied a broad coastal belt in what is now Holland, from the Ems to the Rhine. To the south of them were Frankish tribes. The Swaefe — or Swabians—of whom traces can be found in East Anglia, had by the beginning of the *Adventus Saxonum*, moved to the Middle Rhine, but a remnant of the tribe is believed to have stayed in Schleswig where they occupied a belt of country to the west of the Angles.

When, however, the archaeologists and particularly Thurlow Leeds, pursued their analyses, it became clear that though in some ways these tended to confirm the geographical and cultural divisions of Bede, in others they were curiously confused, and, indeed, reversed. In particular, it is certain that though the various English areas may broadly be either Anglian or Saxon, there were mixed elements in each. This was most pronounced in Middle Anglia, the country immediately to the south and west of, and including most of, the Fenland. Furthermore, though in origin the 'Men of Kent'—i.e. east of the Medway—may be Jutish, yet there are features both in their institutions and particularly in their personal ornaments which point strongly to a source in the Rhineland.

By 1930, Mr. T. D Kendrick, later to be Sir Thomas Kendrick, Director of the British Museum, had begun to publish a series of studies in books and periodicals, in which he offered startling alternative interpretations to what were now orthodox conclusions drawn from this funerary material. Controversy waxed and was further excited by the discoveries of Mr. T. C. Lethbridge, who worked mainly near the Fenland border of East Anglia. It was then, also, that Dr. J. N. L. Myres began that close and careful study of the pagan cremation urns from which he is now drawing far-reaching conclusions.

Much of the controversy centred on the reliability or otherwise of the early settlement history given in the *Anglo-Saxon Chronicle* and the writings of such men as the British Gildas who, in his *De Excidio et Conquesto Britanniae*, a polemic aimed at the native British leaders and written in the second quarter of the sixth century, described somewhat luridly though vaguely the horrors of the Saxon conquest. It cannot be said that these disagreements are yet resolved, but the sudden appearance of a mass of new evidence has enabled, and will further enable, fresh light to be thrown on many of the more doubtful and controversial points, though its discovery has also raised many new questions which are by no means yet fully answered.

It was the late spring of 1939 which saw 'the most remarkable archaeological discovery ever made in England' as Sir Thomas Kendrick was to describe it. This discovery, that of a ship-burial with a wealth of gold, silver, jewellery and other grave-furniture, generally believed to be that of a member of the ancient East Anglian royal house, led to a unique team of archaeologists being drawn together for its complete excavation. For a full realisation of the importance of the find it was unfortunate that, as the investigation progressed, European political tension was increasing and justly had pride of place in the national press. Then, a few days after the last stages of the work were completed, England went to war, the greatest war in her long history.

It is true that some preliminary newspaper reports appeared as the rich finds were brought to light and, as will be described below, these finds came almost at once into the hands of the British Museum. But for the duration of the war, after hasty preliminary treatment, they had necessarily to be deposited in safety from air-raid and other enemy action, so that their full and proper study and publication were much delayed.

Since the end of the war in 1945, work on these finds by the staff of the British Museum has gone steadily forward, notably by Mr. R. L. S. Bruce-Mitford, later Keeper of British and Medieval Antiquities. A vital part was also played by the members of the Laboratory staff under Dr. H. J. Plenderleith and his successor, Dr. A. E. Werner. In this they were assisted by Mr. Herbert Maryon, whose special knowledge of metals and their treatment led to his help being enlisted. As the treatment in the laboratory progressed, many of the objects became available for exhibition. To introduce them to visitors, the British Museum produced in 1947 a well-illustrated *Provisional Guide* which described both the excavation and the grave-goods. This was written by Mr. Bruce-Mitford and has been reprinted several times. He and other scholars, both British and continental, have also published many specialised papers dealing with various aspects of this great discovery. Among these are valuable descriptions by Mr. Maryon of the most important individual objects which have received his particular attention. More yet has to be done and it may be that the final word will not be written for many years to come.

But it has seemed that, so far as the non-specialist reader is concerned, the long break of the wartime years has meant that the full importance and interest of the story has perhaps not been savoured. This book has therefore been written to give a full account of the Sutton Hoo grave: an account comprising the story of the discovery, the details of the excavation, a description of the grave-goods, with the best pieces illustrated in colour and finally, a discussion of the considerable changes brought about in our views of both Early English settlement and political history, and of Early English craftsmanship and artistic accomplishment. In all these ways our enlightenment has been considerable and our evaluation of our Anglo-Saxon forebears greatly enhanced.

This book, then, is not primarily designed for archaeological specialists but for that increasing number of enlightened laymen who are interested both in the realities of the past and in the archaeological activities and techniques which are revealing them to us. It is of necessity greatly indebted to the published papers of specialists, particularly of Mr. C. W. Phillips, now Archaeology Officer to the Ordnance Survey, who directed the major excavation and to those of Mr. R. L. S. Bruce-Mitford. I am also personally indebted to them both for other help.

But in addition to this purely descriptive narrative, I have attempted to do more. In Chapter III I have reviewed the whole troubled question of the design and capabilities of early Anglo-Saxon ships. Our understanding of these vessels has been bedevilled in the past by the occurrence of an odd, apparently square-sterned, boat at Snape in Suffolk, not far from Sutton Hoo, which also contained a seventh-century inhumation burial. However, a careful analysis of the evidence has made it possible to show that this vessel did not depart from the general design inherent in the others, and so to clear up many misunderstandings and uncertainties. By establishing a 'norm' for ships of the period, it has been made possible to discuss more closely in Chapter VII the problem of the crossing from the continent to Britain. The statements in this book have not been documented in detail. But the bibliographical list at the end is fairly full. It includes the more important literature of the subject published in English, as well as a few other works. For those who may wish to follow up some part of the story in greater detail, the books and papers in this list, together with their appended bibliographies of works both in English and other languages, will make this easily possible.

ACKNOWLEDGMENTS

As I have already said, this book could not have been written without the active assistance of Mr. R. L. S. Bruce-Mitford, to whom and to the Trustees of the British Museum I am also grateful for permission to publish many photographs. The Society of Antiquaries of London and Mr. C. W. Phillips have permitted the reproduction of several illustrations from the first account of the excavations. My friend Mr. Norman Smedley, Curator of the Ipswich Museums, has given great help in many ways and to him and to the Museums Committee my thanks are due for permission to publish extracts from their original unpublished records. Those consulted included all Mr. Brown's original field-plans and section-drawings with contemporary annotations by Mr. Guy Maynard. Both Mr. H. E. P. Spencer and Mr. B. J. W. Brown, now or formerly members of the Museum staff, have been most helpful, notably in amplifying details of the happenings of 1938 and 1939.

At my request, my friend Dr. Calvin Wells undertook the first examination of the cremated bones from Barrow No. 3 and, when he recognised the presence of domestic animals' bones, also arranged the supplementary examination by Miss Judith King of the British Museum (Natural History). My friends Mr. and Mrs. J. N. Hutchinson gave great help in the selection and acquisition of Viking-ship photographs from the University Museum of Oslo. I am indebted to Dr. H. Jankuhn of Göttingen University and to Professor Kersten and Dr. Raddatz of the Schleswig-Holsteinisches Landesmuseum für Vor- und Frühgeschichte for photographs of the Nydam ship. For many details of the Utrecht boat, which have not been published in an easily accessible form, I am very grateful to Dr. M. Elisabeth Houtzager, Director of the Centraal Museum der Gemeente Utrecht. Mr. F. T. Baker, Director of the City and County Museum, Lincoln, has generously given me a photograph of the Hough-on-the-Hill whetstone and I am grateful to him and his Committee for permission to publish it.

I am grateful to the Ministry of Works, for whom some of my own fieldwork was done, for permission to use some of my results here. My friend Mr. R. Rainbird Clarke, Curator of the Norwich Museums, has both discussed some of the problems with me and provided several new ideas in his own recently published archaeological survey, *East Anglia* (1960). Both he and my daughter Barbara Green have read my text and clarified many of my ambiguities. To my friends Mr. J. L. Plummer and Messrs. Joseph, John and David Woodhouse, all of the Caister lifeboat crew, past or present, I am greatly indebted for discussing with me at length a variety of technical points. My friend Mr. R. H. Haylett has also given great help in the examination and solution of North Sea problems.

The quoted translations from Anglo-Saxon poetry are taken by permission from Professor R. K. Gordon's *Anglo-Saxon Poetry* (1954), published by Messrs. J. M. Dent and Sons Ltd., in their Everyman Library. Those from Bede's *Ecclesiastical History* are from the same publisher's 1910 Everyman edition. I am also grateful to the editor of *Antiquity* for permission to quote from several articles which have appeared in that magazine and which are listed in the bibliography.

C.G.
1963

Acknowledgment to the undermentioned is due for permission to reproduce the following illustrations: *British Museum*: Figs. 4, 5, 6, 9, 15, 18, 19; Plates I (*a*), II (*b*), VI (*a*), VII (*a*), VIII, IX, X, XI, XII, XIII, XIV, XV. *Society of Antiquaries*: Figs. 3, 7, 8, 12. *Science Museum, London*: Plate IV. *Lincoln Museum*: Plate VI (*b*). Figure 13 is after *C. W. Phillips, Esq., Museum of Prehistory, Schleswig*: Plate III (*a*). *University Museum, Oslo*: Plates II (*a*), III, V (*b*). *Central Museum, Utrecht*: Plate V (*a*).

I

PRELIMINARY ACTIVITY AT

SUTTON HOO

FROM THE Waveney to the Stour, the coastline of Suffolk is broken by several long estuaries, and of these, that of the river Deben is perhaps the most pleasant. Near its head on the west bank, some ten miles upstream from the open coast, stands the small town of Woodbridge and across the river lies the parish of Sutton. Here, on a broad sandy tract of heath, known as Sutton Walks, some 100 feet or more above sea-level, are a group of at least thirteen, and possibly seventeen, barrows. In Britain, barrows of this general type most commonly cover the graves of Bronze Age people of the second millenium B.C. In the succeeding Early Iron Age and Roman periods they were much rarer and in the early Anglo-Saxon period they were uncommon though in some parts of England, pagan Anglo-Saxon burials are not infrequently found as later intrusive burials in the barrows of the Bronze Age.

This barrow-group, known as 'Sutton Mounts', though today concealed from Woodbridge and the river by a nineteenth-century plantation, must formerly have stood boldly outlined on the skyline near the edge of the scarp which slopes down to the water's edge. It lies, too, close to the head of a small combe which provides an easily-sloping access up the scarp. Five of these mounds (numbers 2, 5, 6, 7 and 3, see Fig. 4) form a straight line, while the others are more scattered. The largest ones lie in the western part of the site. Although some have been damaged by later activities on the site, they seem to fall into three sub-groups which may yet prove of some significance. The largest, numbers 1, 2, 3, 7 and 10, are between 85 and 100 feet (26 and 30.5m) in diameter and stand between 6 and 9 feet (1.8 and 2.7m) high. Although Barrow No. 5 has been almost levelled to less than a foot above the surrounding surface, it probably was originally part of this group. Somewhat smaller at a diameter of 60 feet to

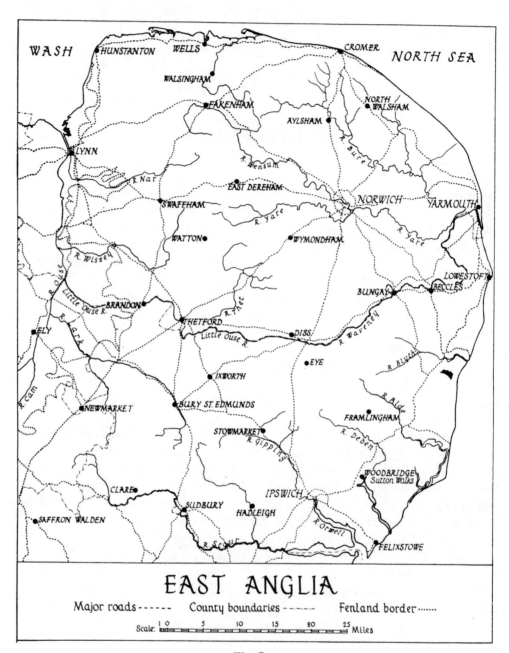

WASH

HUNSTANTON
WELLS
CROMER
NORTH SEA

WALSINGHAM

FAKENHAM
NORTH WALSHAM
AYLSHAM

R. Bure

LYNN

R. Nar

R. Wensum

EAST DEREHAM

SWAFFHAM
NORWICH
YARMOUTH

R. Yare

WATTON
WYMONDHAM

R. Yare

R. Wissey

LOWESTOFT
BECCLES

Ouse

Little Ouse R.

BUNGAY

R. Waveney

ELY
R. Lark
BRANDON
R. Thet
THETFORD
Little Ouse R.
DISS
R. Blyth

EYE

R. Cam
IXWORTH

R. Alde

NEWMARKET
BURY ST. EDMUNDS
FRAMLINGHAM

STOWMARKET
R. Deben
R. Gipping

CLARE
WOODBRIDGE
Sutton Hoo

IPSWICH

SAFFRON WALDEN
SUDBURY
HADLEIGH

R. Orwell

R. Stour
FELIXSTOWE

EAST ANGLIA

Major roads ------   County boundaries ------   Fenland border ······

Scale: 1 0   5   10   15   20   25 Miles

Fig. 2

26

70 feet (18 to 21m) and 2½ to 4 feet (0.75 to 1.2m) high, are Barrow Nos. 4, 6, 8, 9 and 11. Barrow No. 12 probably belongs to this group; it was reduced in height when a field bank was constructed. The remaining five mounds (numbers 13 to 17) are 50 to 60 feet (15 to 18m) in diameter but only a foot or less in height. The identification of these as Anglo-Saxon barrows is, at present, uncertain. Today No. 1, unlike the other mounds, is oval in shape. Excavations carried out in 1967–69 show that it was originally circular like the rest. Part of the western side was dug away in the late Middle Ages for a field

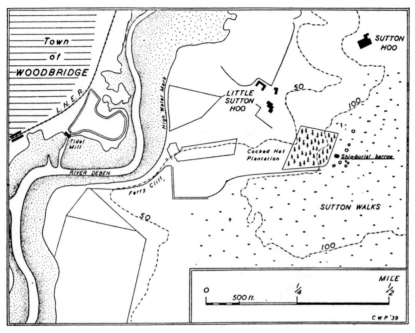

Fig. 3.　Map of the surroundings of the barrows

boundary bank. The apparent centre of the mound therefore came to lie further east than the centre of the original mound. This was a very fortunate occurrence for a hole dug into the new centre by grave robbers in the late sixteenth–early seventeenth century just missed the burial chamber. It is possible that the depressions in the tops of mounds 10 and 7 are the remains of robber trenches; but it is not impossible that they may be due to internal collapse over a long trench in the mound. If so, they may point to other boat burials. An apparently similar depression was noted in mound 2.

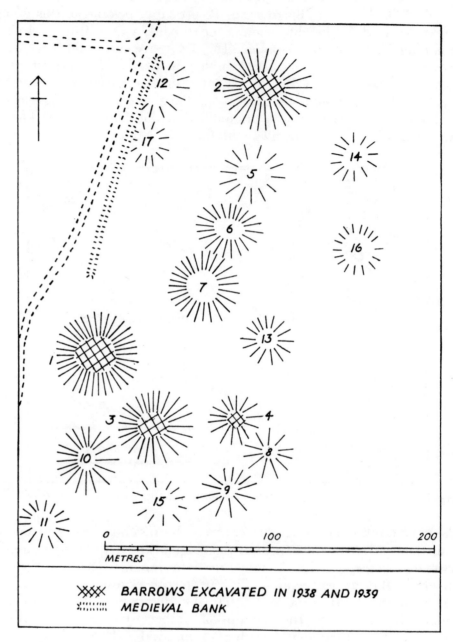

Fig. 4.   Plan of the barrow group

In 1938 the cemetery area was open poor grassland with patches of bracken. The subsoil is sand with only a little gravel and it was thought that the area had been open heath since prehistoric times. However the opportunity was taken during the 1965/66 and 1970 investigations of the site to study the soil profiles under mounds 1 and 5. This showed that there had been considerable changes in the vegetation and agricultural use of the site. Pollen from buried old soil indicated pastoral farming on a forest clearing during part of the second millenium B.C. This was perhaps contemporary with the Early Bronze Age occupation of the site. Above this was sand, in places wind-blown, and another, disturbed, soil. Pollen evidence suggested that the barrows had been constructed directly on arable farmland.

In 1938, most of the barrows lay just within the estate of the late Mrs. E. M. Pretty, J. P., and one (No. 11) being over the boundary of an estate belonging to the Duke of Rutland. Mrs. Pretty had frequently expressed curiosity about the contents of these barrows and at last arranged with Mr. Guy Maynard, at that time Curator of the Ipswich Museum, to have some of them opened. On Mr. Maynard's staff was Mr. B. J. W. Brown, whose primary duties were field reconnaissance and test-digging in the county. To Mr. Brown, therefore, fell the privilege of testing these barrows by excavation. Visits were also paid from time to time by Mr. H. E. P. Spencer, then geologist in the museum, who also kept certain records in addition to those made from day to day by Mr. Brown.

During that year, three of the barrows, Nos. 2, 3 and 4, were opened. Mrs. Pretty had at first expressed a wish for work to begin on No. 1, the highest of all. But wisely and most fortunately as it transpired, Mr. Maynard dissuaded her by pointing out that some evidence of their date and structural method should first be obtained from some of the smaller—and presumably less important— members of the group. In consequence work was begun on No. 3, which was approximately 85 feet (26m) in diameter and about 8 feet (2.4m) high. Before digging began an oval hollow in the top of the mound was noted. Mr. Brown began digging his trench from the western side, starting well outside the mound. He found a shallow ditch which surrounded the mound. In the middle of the mound he found a burial pit, slightly off centre, which had been dug into the hard yellow sand. It was filled with a reddish sand and separated from an upper fill of mixed sand and stones. The layer separating the two fills was a saucer-shaped black soil thought at first to be the remains of a hearth but later identified as an old turf line. At the bottom of the burial pit he found the decayed remains of a long wooden tray. Its corners were not sharply angular, but slightly rounded. The substance of the wood had long been destroyed by decay and so the tray could not be lifted. But its essential structure was fairly clear and adequate measurements could be taken. Its overall length was 5 ½ feet (1.65m) and its breadth some 22 inches (56cm). All round ran a raised rim and the whole shape showed that this tray was a great slab of timber with its upper surface hollowed. It was, in effect, a very shallow dugout coffin without a lid.

At the western end of the tray, just inside the raised lip, lay a heap of cremated bones. Nearby were some pieces of decorated bone, a piece of decorated grey stone, a potsherd and a small bronze object. At the east end of the tray was another heap of burnt bones, some of which had spilled onto the grave floor. Also on the grave floor lay a single piece of decorated bone. It was the potsherd, decorated with incised patterns, which determined immediately the period of the burial. It came from the shoulder of a large hand-made urn of pagan Anglo-Saxon type. The dating of this potsherd was confirmed by the presence of a very rusted axehead which lay on the floor of the grave close to the south-western corner of the tray. This axehead was a Frankish type of throwing-axe or 'francisca'. The socket still held a fragment of its wooden haft. The pointed tips of the blades were missing but it has been possible to reconstruct the original blade shape from its similarity to an axe in France. Two other pieces useful for dating the grave were the bronze object which turned out to be the lid of a ewer or jug made in the Eastern Mediterranean, and the broken piece of grey stone, carved in relief with a winged figure, perhaps a Victory. Similar pieces have been found in Sweden in the West Mound at Old Uppsala. An origin in Sassanian Iran has been suggested for these. The date of this burial is likely to be between A.D. 550 and 600. It is difficult to be certain if it had been robbed or not.

Many, if not all, of the calcined bone fragments were preserved and have more recently been fully assessed by competent persons. Unfortunately the remains, as they are now preserved, cannot be assigned to one or the other of the two deposits and have been mixed. Many are so badly crushed that their identification is quite impossible. Others have been identified as the remains of an adult male and a horse. One of the pieces of decorated bone was identified as a fragment of a bone comb. The other pieces were the remains of veneer from a wooden casket. Both types of objects are found in Anglo-Saxon graves.

Barrow No. 2 was the next to be opened. It was about 100 feet (30.5m) in diameter and between 7 and 8 feet (2 and 2.4m) high, and again a shallow ditch was found to have surrounded the mound. A broad trench was driven into the mound slightly off centre and then expanded into a rectangular area some 18 feet by 24 feet (5.4 by 7.3m). This clearance exposed a long pointed-oval grave-area which, when emptied, proved to be a grave-pit containing the remains of a boat. Most of the wood of the boat had long ago decayed, but its presence was shown by a dark smear in the sand-filling of the pit. Also present were the rusty nodules which had once been the clench-nails of a clinker-built vessel. The pit which had been dug to take the boat had been nicely judged for size and, except at the stern which touched the end of the pit, showed a gap of about 1 foot all round at the presumed gunwale level. It is possible, however, that the stemhead of the boat had projected above the original surface and had been destroyed either before or during the preliminary uncovering. The boat was pointed at the western end but the eastern end, presumably the stern, was broad and straight like that of a modern dinghy. The possible significance of this will be discussed later.

Mr. Brown found evidence that grave robbers in the past had dug into the boat and disturbed and looted the contents. Only a few objects remained scattered throughout the vessel. But these were enough to show that the boat had contained a man's richly furnished inhumation burial. That the grave had been disturbed was clear when Mr. Brown found fragments of glass and a fragment of bone high in the fill. The quality of these pieces showed that the boat had originally held a richly furnished male burial. Although no skeleton was found, the end of a sword blade, still with part of the scabbard remaining and two mounts, probably from a shield, indicate the sex of the burial. These two mounts, one a gold-plated bronze disc covered with interlace ornament of early seventh century date and a gilded bronze strip ending in a dragon's head, help to date the burial to the early seventh century. This date is further confirmed by pieces of a blue glass vessel, probably made in Kent about A.D. 600. Some fragments of thin silver-gilt foil decorated with stamped animal ornament are of considerable interest. They are parts of triangular decorative mounts from a large drinking horn similar to that found in the 1939 great ship burial. The same dies were used for the mounts on both drinking horns. At the east end of the boat were a number of pieces of iron including bands.

These have subsequently been identified as the fittings of a large wooden tub, 19 inches (48cm) high and 20 inches (51cm) in diameter at the rim. Beneath the barrow Mr. Brown found a number of sherds of Bronze Age pottery associated with a hearth. He also found a tubular segmented bead of faience, of a type commoner in Wiltshire than East Anglia.

The last barrow to be opened in 1938 was No. 4. It was a broad, rather flattened mound, marked at its centre by a funnel-shaped hollow which penetrated almost to the original surface-level. A 5 foot (1.5m) trench was cut to the centre of the mound where a 14 foot (4.2m) square exposed the centre grave dug into the original surface.

This grave, a long oval pit some 7 feet long by 3 feet wide (2m by 0.9m), with its long axis almost east-west, contained at its eastern end a heap of cremated bone fragments. There was also a thin scatter of burnt bone fragments over much of the grave-base. With the bones at the east end were many small fragments of thin bronze sheeting which, it was thought, were the remains of a bronze bowl largely destroyed by corrosion. Some of these fragments carried traces, impressed in the corroded surface, of finely-woven fabric.

Mr. Brown's exposed sections made it fairly clear that the funnel-shaped hollow in the overlying mound had been left in the past by barrow-robbers who had dropped a central shaft into the original grave. It is possible, though not certain, that the scatter of bones was due to their disturbance. What is more, it seems probable that grave-furniture, other than the corroded bronze bowl, was removed by them, though of the nature and extent of this hypothetical loot there was no trace. It was also noted that the barrow had originally been surrounded by a ditch.

All the finds which were made during the season's digging were given by Mrs. Pretty to the Ipswich Museum. To an archaeologist who specialised in the period the discoveries, particularly of what seemed to be a burial in a boat and the cremation burials with the tray, were of great interest and importance and seemed to point to new possibilities in the study of Anglo-Saxon times. But the loose finds transferred to the museum were not very spectacular and the other results had not been widely publicised, so that their real significance was at that time hardly suspected.

Mrs. Pretty, however, was determined to know more about the contents of her barrows. She held further discussions with Mr. Maynard and, in Mr. Brown's own words,[1] 'On April 4, 1939, I received a letter from Mr. Guy Maynard containing the following: "If you would like another spell at Sutton Hoo, Mrs. Pretty is willing to resume work on the barrows." On Monday, May 8, I arrived at Sutton Hoo and had an interview with Mrs. E. M. Pretty, during which arrangements were made regarding personnel and equipment for the excavation. We then went to the barrows and upon my asking Mrs. Pretty which mound she would like opened, she pointed to the largest of the group (Tumulus 1) and said: "What about this?" and I replied that it would be quite all right for me. After a preliminary survey of the mound, work was commenced in the afternoon and the technique decided upon as similar to that adopted for dealing with the tumuli explored in 1938.' So simply and almost casually was the decision made which led to the dramatic finding of the unique treasure-ship.

The story may now be continued in Mr. Brown's own words. 'The original form of the barrow had been greatly altered by various disturbances; on the west many tons of material had been removed and had it not been prevented by the late Colonel Frank Pretty, who turned down a proposal to use material from the mound to make up the farmyards, more would have gone, while on the east material had also been taken for bunkers of a private golf course. Also, evidence was forthcoming from a game-keeper who had dug into the mound at the request of a former owner of the estate in the hope of finding treasure. Lastly there was damage from the rabbits which had burrowed into the mound for centuries. The mound which before excavation presented a hogback appearance, especially when observed from the west, was in plan an elongated oval. . . .

'An initial or exploratory trench 6 feet wide was cut east to west across the mound down to the old ground surface, care being taken to note any inequality in the level of the sand which might serve to indicate a grave beneath and also for ship-nails in view of the data obtained from the 1938 excavations. On May 11, I was able to deduce with certainty the existence of a pit or grave below the old ground surface and explained the indications to Mrs. Pretty and that our trench was practically following the same alignment. I proceeded to

---

[1] I am grateful to the Committee and Curator of the Ipswich Museum who gave me access to their files and permitted me to make extracts from notes prepared at the time of the excavation.

33

widen our exploratory trench to 12 feet to admit of clearing the grave pit.

'The first find was a loose ship-nail and then five others in position. We were definitely at one end of a ship which was protruding a little above the old ground surface which here had been much disturbed by rabbits, fortunately without destroying the end or displacing the iron nails which remained in their original places. It was at first thought that this was the stern end of the ship and that its bow would be pointing to the Deben, but it was not until the vessel had been almost completely excavated that this point was elucidated and that her bow was known to point to the east.

'From now on extreme care had to be practised and the ship's interior was gradually cleared, frame by frame, with small tools and bare hands, the spoil being removed with the kitchen dustpan from Little Sutton. As soon as the rust of a ship's nail showed in the sand or the black and grey dust from wood decomposition, these features were left. As work progressed and the ship gradually opened out, drastic cut-backs were made and timbering with terraces became necessary to avoid landslides; the cutting through the mound proper assumed a width of 40 feet. It now became evident from the indications that a larger craft than the Snape ship was to be expected with a strong possibility of a length of at least 50 feet.

'While I worked at clearing the vessel's interior, the men were engaged in clearing the top layers and cutting away the mound-content, section by section, towards the west and widening the cutting. A careful lookout was kept for anything of interest which might turn up, but the only finds were Bronze Age sherds and part of a stone axe.'

On May 30, Mr. Brown found, at about the old surface-level, the remains of a fire of sticks, a broken piece of animal bone and a part of a tiger-ware jug. A later analysis of the exposed section showed that this barrow, too, had been sampled in the past by other barrow-robbers than Mr. Brown's gamekeeper. A shaft had been dropped to the original surface level and these remains lay at its bottom, suggesting that the robbers had lunched there before they refilled their shaft. It was indeed the ancient mutilation of the mound which led to this assault on the barrow being fruitless. For they had dropped their shaft in what they thought was the centre of the mound but, owing to its mutilation, they were well to one side of the original centre-point and so failed to find the underlying burial-chamber (see Fig. 6).

The tiger-ware vessel shows that this attempt was probably made late in the sixteenth or early in the seventeenth century. The rather daring suggestion has been made that it could have been the work of Dr. John Dee, a well-known alchemist and astrologer of Elizabethan days. Though the evidence is rather vague, he appears to have been commissioned to search for gold on behalf of the queen and a record of an attempt he made to find gold at Beeleigh in Essex is preserved in the Maldon Corporation Records. But, whether official or private in origin, the search failed and the grave-goods remained intact.

By June 11, Mr. Brown had cleared to the eleventh frame of the ship. Here traces of a former timber barrier began to show, together with pieces of bronze and iron. From this it began to be inferred, as was later shown to be true, that in the central portion of the ship a burial-chamber had been constructed. Though it was anticipated that this could hardly have survived intact, the remains already seen showed that something at least was there and the very difficult problem of dealing with this part of the ship began to be considered.

It was just at this time that Mr. C. W. Phillips paid a short visit to the site. Mr. Phillips, then a lecturer at Selwyn College, Cambridge, and an archaeologist of considerable standing, quickly realised the potentialities and difficulties of the task before the excavators and strongly advised a halt while the British Museum and Office of Works were consulted. This advice was wisely followed and the discussions took place. Finally it was agreed that the work should be finished by the Office of Works (as it then was) and Mr. Phillips was invited by them to take charge on their behalf. For a detailed survey of the ship when it should be possible, the Science Museum agreed to provide a specialist for the purpose. And so we have Mr. Brown's note that 'On July 8, Mr. C. W. Phillips arrived. He would, I was informed, now supervise the work on behalf of the Office of Works, etc., while I would act as his assistant, Mrs. Pretty consenting to the arrangement.'

The problems which now confronted Mr. Phillips were of some magnitude. Had he directed the excavations from the beginning, he would probably have adopted a rather different method of dissecting the mound. But the work had progressed too far for any significant change to be practicable, and he could only continue to drive a broad trench through the body of the mound, leaving ample space on either side both for safety and as a working platform. Mr. Brown's good workmanship and care had made this possible and all that was required here was further extension to meet the increased complexity of the task. But it was not just a matter of exposing and emptying the ship.

35

Before the central overburden could be fully removed it had so to be analysed that as full a picture as possible of the ruined burial-chamber could be obtained. Furthermore, the previous excavations had shown that the condition of the deposits in the ship would probably not be good. To work out their full story, specialist treatment would be required.

When it became clear that the chamber did, in fact, contain an untouched deposit which would need the best available skill and experience for its removal, other leading archaeologists came forward to give their services. Much of the work of removing the grave-goods was done by Mr. W. F. Grimes, later Professor of Prehistoric Archaeology and later Director of the Institute of Archaeology in the University of London. Other important work was done by Mr. Stuart Piggott, later Abercromby Professor of Prehistory in the University of Edinburgh, and his wife. The late Mr. O. G. S. Crawford, then Archaeology Officer to the Ordnance Survey and Editor of *Antiquity*, made a complete photographic record of the emptying of the burial chamber; other valuable photographic work was done by Miss M. K. Lack and Miss B. Wagstaff. Many other workers of standing, including members of the British Museum staff, gave help at critical moments; they included Professor F. E. Zeuner of the Institute of Archaeology, who analysed the soils and substance of the barrow, and staff from the Science Museum made a survey of the boat. It is fair to say that never before in the history of archaeology had there been such a team of specialists working together in the field.

Mr. Phillips bore another responsibility which rarely falls to an archaeologist in the field. This stemmed from the bullion value of many of the finds. With quantities of gold, silver and jewellery still in the ground, the working team endeavoured to observe a discreet reticence about their findings. But of course it was impossible to prevent some rumour of their quality spreading. And so, to prevent unauthorised raiding, a police-guard had to be provided. This surprising variant of normal police work was ably organised by Mr. G. E. Staunton, O.B.E., Chief Constable of East Suffolk; his men of the Woodbridge Division, like the dragon in Northern story, guarded the hoard of gold.

II

THE SHIP-BARROW EXCAVATION

WHEN MR. PHILLIPS took over the direction of the excavation, Mr. Brown and his team had just cleared from the bows of the ship to the eleventh frame, where they had seen what appeared to be a timber partition across the interior of the vessel. From this it had been inferred, as has been said, that the central part had contained some sort of burial-chamber, built to protect the body and its accompanying grave-goods. This inference was later shown to be true but, as what evidently had been a substantial timber partition now showed merely as a 'slight dark discoloration in the sand not more than a quarter of an inch thick . . . only the most careful watch made it possible to get any idea of what had formerly existed'.

In order to ascertain the structural detail of this chamber, a different method of clearance was adopted. The sides of the cutting in the mound were further cut back and the central area, for a length of some 25 feet (7.5m), was cut away horizontally. This was done with long-handled coal shovels with which the sand could be shaved away in very thin slices. Any trace of discoloration in the area could then be noted and, as successive slices were removed, could be followed downward in whatever direction it might trend. By some trick of the packing or of the collapse, one fragment of wood, apparently from this structure, had not been disintegrated by decay. This carbonised oak was left in position on a supporting pillar of sand and so provided a 'control section' for the rest of the chamber. It also showed that the roof of the chamber had been covered with turf, though whether this was a special covering or just a part of the ordinary structure of the over-lying mound was not quite clear. Mr. Phillips thought that the first explanation might well be true.

Excavation by this careful shaving-method was soon to be rewarded for, some 17½ feet (5.25m) to the west of the first cross-partition, the second was exposed, again as a slight stain in the sand. The extent of the chamber having now been defined, the clearance progressed more confidently and quickly gave further results. On the south side of the chamber, another line of decayed wood appeared, this time running parallel to the ship's side. When followed downward, this was seen to slope outward towards the side of the ship. A column of filling, containing this sloping line, was left standing for a time until the rest of the clearance had been finished. It could then be seen that, when the sloping roof of the chamber had collapsed, a small part on the

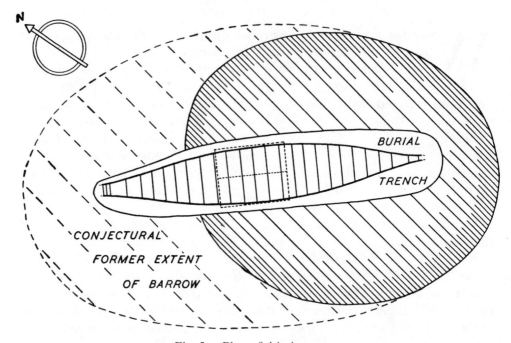

Fig. 5.   Plan of ship-barrow

south side had remained in position. From this, of course, it was possible with some confidence to calculate the pitch and, from that, the height of the roof. This section is illustrated in Fig. 7 and the reconstructed line of the roof in Fig. 6. The two ends of the chamber, therefore, were gabled, the peak standing some 12 feet (3.6m) above the keel-plank, with the eaves of the roof resting on the ship's gunwale.

At a later stage of the work, the grave-goods were seen to be overlain in places by decayed planking, apparently fallen fragments of

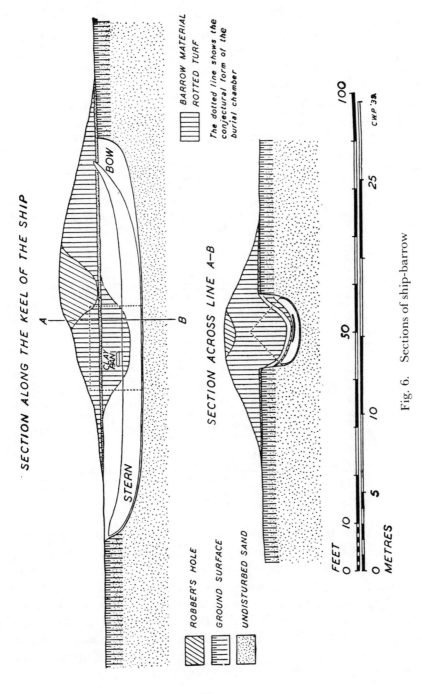

SECTION ALONG THE KEEL OF THE SHIP

BOW

STERN

A

CLAY PAN

B

ROBBER'S HOLE

GROUND SURFACE

UNDISTURBED SAND

BARROW MATERIAL

ROTTED TURF

The dotted line shows the conjectural form of the burial chamber

SECTION ACROSS LINE A–B

FEET
0   5   10

METRES
0   5   10   25   50   100

CWP '39.

Fig. 6.   Sections of ship-barrow

Sutton Hoo

the roof. These remnants lay pointing in two directions at right angles to each other. From this it was inferred that the roof itself was of double thickness, one layer of planks running from gable to gable, the other from eaves to ridge. No trace of a door could be discerned at either end and nothing could be inferred of the timber framework which must have supported the planked ends and roof. At one end, however, a rusted angle-iron was found; this perhaps had a place in the structure. And later, when the burial deposits had been cleared, a number of metal cleats forming a line on either side of the ship's floor

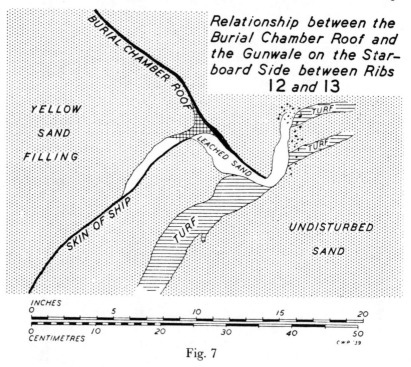

Relationship between the Burial Chamber Roof and the Gunwale on the Starboard Side between Ribs 12 and 13

Fig. 7

was seen; they may also have served some structural purpose in this hut. Sawn-off scraps of planking were also found on the flooring; these, it was thought, were fallen pieces left by the chamber-builders. When the mound had been constructed over the chamber, the latter of course had not been filled with sand. The filling removed by the excavators was that which had fallen in after the collapse of the roof which seems not to have happened until many years after the burial. Outside the chamber, however, the ends of the ship had been completely filled at an early stage in the erection of the mound.

40

Above the grave-goods in this collapsed chamber-filling was found a curious clay structure. This was an oval slab of clay with a saucer-shaped hollow in its upper surface. The slab was about 36 inches by 18 inches by 5 inches (90cm x 46cm x 12.5cm) deep and showed no traces of fire, so that it could not have been used as a hearth. It was, therefore, suggested that after the lower part of the mound had been built around and over the chamber, this receptacle had been laid above the roof where, perhaps, it received libations as part of the burial ceremony. No exact parallel for this clay-pan is known. However, more recent studies suggest it formed naturally after the collapse of the chamber.

The emptying of the lower part of the burial-chamber now proceeded rapidly and soon the first objects began to show above the damp sandy filling. In Fig. 9 will be seen a plan of their distribution; it appears, as Mr. Phillips has said, 'in the form of a large letter H, with crossbar of exaggerated length.' The work now demanded even greater care and forethought than before. Gold, as is well known, is little subject to chemical corrosion and the objects of gold in the hoard were in essentially good condition. But the other objects, whether of silver, bronze, iron, or leather and woven fabric, were in parlous condition, partly due to the corrosion of the damp sand and partly to the pressure of the overlying collapsed roof and mound.

The method of clearing now had to be changed and the long-handled shovel gave place to paint-brush and packing needle. With these new tools, the topmost layer of sand on and around each object was removed, exposing the damper sand below. This soon dried in the hot sun and was then removed in similar fashion until the object was completely exposed and undercut as far as was possible. Such precise treatment, with its resulting slow progress, was very necessary as, in their flimsy and corroded condition, the slightest adhesive contact of wet sand increased the strains on the thin and distorted metals and so lessened the chances of removing each object without further damage.

But some of the objects could not be allowed to dry in this way. Leather, the gourds and fabrics, as well as other things, began to distort and crumble as they dried and so these were frequently removed in a block and, wrapped carefully in damp coverings often of moss, were then transported to be individually cleaned and sorted when they had reached the laboratory. Though this meant that the precise nature of each object was not recognised at the time and the very existence of some was not suspected, the true shapes and relationships were better able to be worked out in the more suitable environment of the laboratory, where also were the resources required for the rapid treatment which sometimes was so urgently needed during the unpacking.

Not only in the uncovering and packing was this care exercised; equally important was the record-making as the objects emerged. For, grouped and disintegrated as they were, it was frequently difficult or impossible to be sure to which object a detached fragment might belong. For example, during the uncovering of the group under the great silver dish, a fluted bowl lay by the remains of a leather bag. This bag was equipped with a 'strap fitted with bronze buckle and slider to pass round it for support when full' and to this bag was also attributed a pair of silver handles. But later, in the laboratory, it was seen that the silver handles were, in fact, a part of the fluted bowl, from which they had become detached. And so, stage by stage and detail by detail, sketches and descriptive notes were multiplied. In this work the camera also proved its importance. While this part of the clearance was in progress Mr. O. G. S. Crawford made his very full photographic record, capturing each group as, little by little, they were exposed and so supplementing the notes with a permanent pictorial record of the precise position of each fragment. In the subsequent work of restoration all this was to prove invaluable.

Much of the work of removing the objects from the chamber, as has been said, was done by Mr. W. F. Grimes. In 1940 he published a description of that work, so that we may now follow him into the excavated pit and see what he saw. He says that 'the dominant feature in my first view of the ship was a great three-foot purple-grey disk; the silver dish, beneath which the lip of at least one other vessel was promise of more treasure to come. Other things there were already exposed—especially the two bronze bowls at the southwest corner of the burial deposit. But the urgent interest was centred on the dish and on the problem of whether it could be lifted entire, or whether steps should be taken by means of drawings and photographs to record its complete character before the hazardous work of lifting it began.'

Now this dish was lying right way up and it could be seen that it bore a complicated engraved ornament (see Chapter IV) so that, to record it fully, all this ornament would have had to be drawn and photographed in detail, a task of great difficulty. Fortunately, so much preliminary work was judged to be unnecessary as 'the metal was thick and seemed to be strong, in spite of a crack along one side.' The dish was safely lifted on July 26 and, as Mr. Grimes says, 'Beneath it was an assortment of articles, most of them in a fragile and parlous state, the recording, removal, and packing of which took the undivided attention of all working on the site.'

In the fluted bowl, for example, were several small cups with metal mounts; the cups themselves were of wood. Warped and damaged as they were, no delay in their treatment could be allowed, sun-drying in particular being the greatest danger. Into boxes they went at once, tightly packed in damp moss, which served to maintain their condition until laboratory treatment made them safe. Immediately under the great dish and around the fluted bowl were masses of leather, flock-like material which later proved to be goose down and woven textile fabrics; the leather objects included bags and shoes. All these were decayed, the cloth being very rotten; to permit them to dry would have meant their complete loss. They were accordingly placed at once in bowls of water where they were kept until they could be properly packed for travelling. Also here were a small silver cup and what later proved to be a silver ladle, a small ivory gamespiece and two badly decayed bronze hanging-bowls.

When all these varied objects had been removed, it was seen that they had been resting on a great wooden tray, a part only of which remained. On this, protected by the cloth and leather, were found an iron axe and a mass of rusted iron chain-mail. The tray fragment, some at least of which was still in condition to be lifted, was finally dealt with. As so much of the wood in the ship and chamber had completely decayed, it was rather surprising that a part of this tray had, comparatively speaking, survived; it is thought that this was due largely to the protection given by the leather and cloth over which lay the great dish.

The greatest concentration of grave-goods was certainly that at the west end of the chamber; they lay packed close to the wooden wall. The first to be found was a giant whetstone with carved and bronze-decorated ends. This, of course, was in sound condition and was lifted with ease, but soon, more complex objects began to be exposed. Still closer to the wall lay a mass of rusted iron which, as it was cleared, was revealed as a long iron rod with various structural attachments. Though so heavily rusted, this 'lamp-stand' as it was named, was by no means destroyed and, when completely cleared of sand, was quite strong enough to be lifted by three persons on to a plank; on this it was suitably supported by packing and made fast. Near the upper part of this stand there lay an iron ring on which was a beautifully-modelled

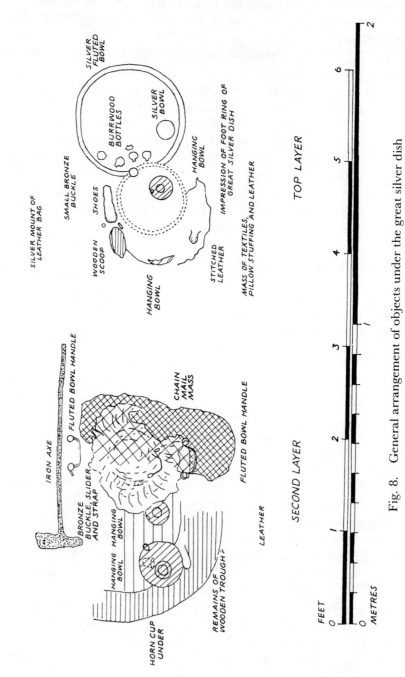

SILVER MOUNT OF LEATHER BAG

SMALL BRONZE BUCKLE

SILVER FLUTED BOWL

BURRWOOD BOTTLES

SILVER BOWL

SHOES

WOODEN SCOOP

HANGING BOWL

IMPRESSION OF FOOT RING OF GREAT SILVER DISH

HANGING BOWL

STITCHED LEATHER

MASS OF TEXTILES, PILLOW STUFFING AND LEATHER

TOP LAYER

IRON AXE

FLUTED BOWL HANDLE

CHAIN MAIL MASS

BRONZE BUCKLE, SLIDER AND STRAP

FLUTED BOWL HANDLE

HANGING HANGING BOWL BOWL

LEATHER

HORN CUP UNDER

REMAINS OF WOODEN TROUGH?

SECOND LAYER

FEET

0   1   2   3   4   5   6

METRES

0   1   2

Fig. 8.   General arrangement of objects under the great silver dish

image in bronze of an antlered stag. It was at the time thought perhaps to be a helmet-crest.

On the other side of the stand was the collapsed ruin of a large wooden bucket with iron mountings. But sufficient of this was left to make its removal as a unit worth while. When the sand was cleared away, the remnants of the bucket were swathed in strong webbing. By slow degrees a thin iron plate was then slipped beneath, space for it being cleared by trowelling. It was now realised that the plate was too thin to carry the weight without bending, so the whole complex of plate and swaddled bucket was picked up on a spade and lifted on to a strong wooden base where it was made secure without any of its parts having suffered serious disturbance.

To the south of this bucket lay a complex group composed apparently of two bronze bowls, one inside the other, and a number of spear and angon heads of iron. The latter were even resting in one of the handles of the outer bowl with which they were in contact. Accordingly, the whole group was lifted as a single unit, to be treated and disengaged in the laboratory. Later, about 7 feet (2m) away, iron ferrules thought to be from the butts of spear-shafts were also found; subsequent work suggests they belong to the angons.

To the east of the bucket lay, in Mr. Grimes' words, 'a smudge of purple indicating silver, of which we had been conscious for some time. It was roughly circular in shape and near it was what appeared to be the end of a slender moulded bar.' Cleaning this silver was perhaps one of the most difficult tasks undertaken by Mr. Grimes. It proved finally to be a nest of inverted silver bowls and the silver rod was the handle of a spoon, below which lay another similar spoon. One of the bowls had slipped from the pile and was completely disintegrated, so that a photographic record only was possible. The remainder were lifted *en bloc* on an iron plate similar to that under the bucket and packed to be isolated in the laboratory. At first it was thought that this pack contained eight bowls, but later analysis proved that it held nine, six only of which were in good condition. Altogether therefore a stack of no less than ten of these bowls was deposited in the grave.

Near the north end of the stand was what Mr. Grimes himself claimed was 'perhaps the most intricate piece of cleaning: that of the remains of the shield', though this task, which took almost a whole day, he dismissed in comparatively few words. 'The central feature was the massive boss, which was solid and unlikely to cause trouble.

But radiating irregularly from it were several richly decorated bronze mounts: some of almost paper thinness, some face upwards, some reversed, at all angles and presenting a picture of complete confusion. . . . To add to the difficulties this complex was partly covered with the remains of a fine wooden object ornamented with gold leaf. None of the material of the shield itself appeared to remain. The *umbo* was lifted without difficulty, but freeing the various adhesions of the mounts was a slow and tedious business. Each was lifted separately on two or more trowels after it had been drawn in on the plan.' In this very brief account, slight mention only is made of what was thought to be a thin wooden 'tray' with gilt gesso edging and animal-head decoration, which seemed to overlie the heavier mountings of the shield. It was not until the whole complex began to be analysed and studied in the British Museum that these, too, were seen to be a part of the shield itself. Near the tray were some fragments thought to be ivory. These were later identified as ivory gaming pieces.

To the east of the shield lay what was called the 'nucleus' of a helmet. It is not certain where this helmet was originally placed, for fragments of it were scattered over a much larger area, and it seems that it must have been damaged and dispersed by the fall of the roof. To the present writer it seems not unlikely that it may have hung on the gabled west wall of the chamber, to be flung down and broken when the first fall happened. But sufficient remained to make its unusual character evident and the description of the gathered fragments, made when they were unpacked (see p. 77), and the final reconstruction, serve to show its magnificence.

Close to the silver bowls and just to the south of the centre-line of the ship, were an iron blade and a sword. The blade was heavily rusted and appeared to be a scramasax, a characteristic weapon of the times, best described as a small cutlass. The sword itself had been a magnificent weapon, but it had been seriously damaged by the fall of the roof, as well as by rusting. It apparently had a wooden scabbard, bound with fabric at the lower end. Its hilt was decorated with gold and garnets.

Both over the sword and between it and the 'helmet nucleus' were scattered the gold and jewelled objects which formed the most costly part of the deposit; they were described by Mr. Phillips as 'the finest collection of Anglo-Saxon jewellery yet known'. These pieces comprised buckles, purse, clasps and small mounts of various types which, it seems, must have been attached to a complex leather harness made to

46

be worn by a man, though its disposition was not what it would have been if worn by a body at the time of the burial. As Mr. Phillips records, most of these pieces lay face downward and he suggests that the harness may originally have been hanging up in the chamber, to be thrown down at the time of the collapse. The beautifully jewelled purse contained a number of Merovingian (Frankish) gold coins and two small gold ingots. These coins, as we shall see, were to provide a fairly close date for the burial.

Immediately to the east of the jewellery lay another complex which again, owing to its sadly decayed condition, was lifted *en bloc* to be treated and analysed in the laboratory. This complex had probably been in part protected by a layer of roof-planking, but at the time of the fall, the wood must have pressed the underlying objects flat. These very puzzling objects were finally seen to be a collection of drinking vessels with silver-gilt mounts. In two, traces of the original horn were preserved. Others showed merely as flat triangles like the 'rays' of a starfish and there was some indication that these vessels had originally been covered in cloth. The metal itself of the mounts had been converted to a salt of the element, but enough remained for the designs, or some of them, to be recorded, though permanent preservation was not possible.

On the south side of the chamber, a single object lay outside the H-pattern made by the others. This was a second iron-bound wooden bucket, generally similar to that lifted from the west end. And, near to the east end, close to the great silver dish, lay a wheel-turned pottery bottle and a small iron lamp. Finally, across the eastern end lay a further group of large objects. These comprised three bronze cauldrons of different sizes, a large iron-bound wooden bucket or tub and a mass of iron chainwork and bars. Of the wooden bucket nothing remained but the very rusty binding. The largest of the three cauldrons was much crushed, but the metal was still in fairly good condition, giving some hope of its future restoration. But the smaller cauldrons were so crushed and corroded that the thin sheet bronze of which they were made had fallen away into 'hundreds of small pieces', leaving little hope of a successful reconstruction.

Now in the layout of these grave-goods, the 'place of honour' would seem to have been on the central line towards the west end, below the gold and jewelled harness-fittings. Here the buried body would be expected to lie. But neither here nor, indeed, anywhere in the chamber did the excavators discover any trace of a body. It is this apparent

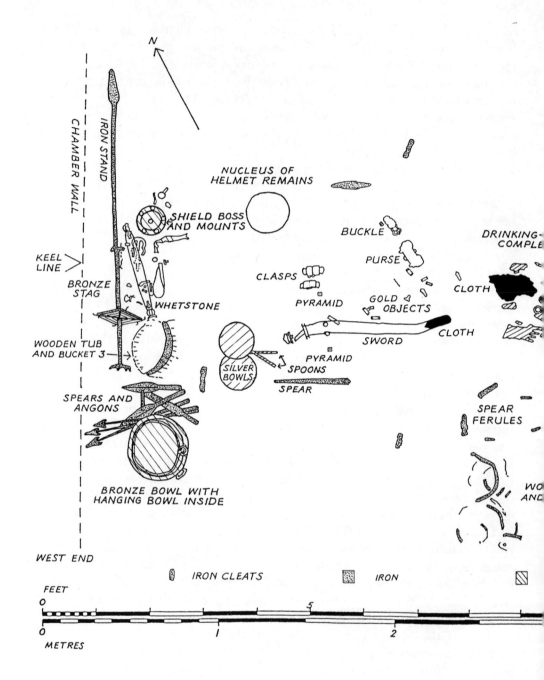

N

CHAMBER WALL

IRON STAND

NUCLEUS OF
HELMET REMAINS

SHIELD BOSS
AND MOUNTS

BUCKLE

DRINKING-
COMPLE

KEEL
LINE

PURSE

BRONZE
STAG

CLASPS

PYRAMID

CLOTH

GOLD &
OBJECTS

WHETSTONE

CLOTH

WOODEN TUB
AND BUCKET 3

SWORD

SILVER
BOWLS

PYRAMID
SPOONS

SPEAR

SPEARS AND
ANGONS

SPEAR
FERULES

WO
AND

BRONZE BOWL WITH
HANGING BOWL INSIDE

WEST END

IRON CLEATS

IRON

FEET

0

5

0

1

2

METRES

Fig. 9.   Plan of the funeral deposit

48

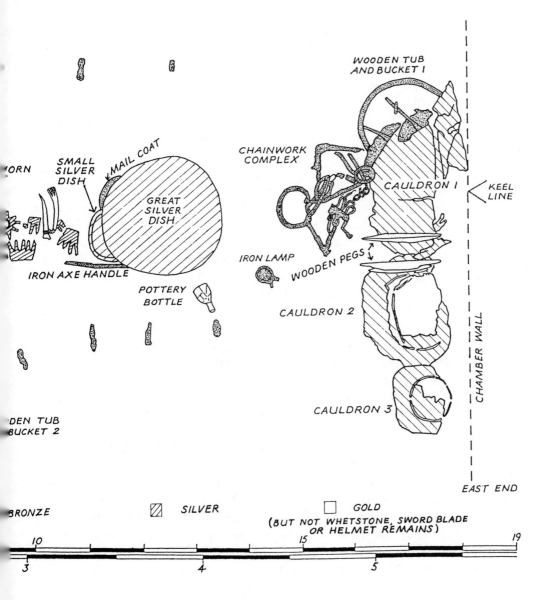

ORN

SMALL
SILVER
DISH

MAIL COAT

GREAT
SILVER
DISH

IRON AXE HANDLE

POTTERY
BOTTLE

WOODEN TUB
AND BUCKET I

CHAINWORK
COMPLEX

CAULDRON I

KEEL
LINE

IRON LAMP

WOODEN PEGS

CAULDRON 2

CHAMBER WALL

CAULDRON 3

DEN TUB
BUCKET 2

EAST END

BRONZE

SILVER

GOLD
(BUT NOT WHETSTONE, SWORD BLADE
OR HELMET REMAINS)

10   15   19

3   4   5

49

absence of a body which has led to much debate. This is discussed in Chapter V.

The burial-chamber was now empty, but work did not cease as the remaining third of the boat, aft of the chamber, had still to be emptied of its filling of sand. Here the work was lightened, for most of the mound in this area had already disappeared. This clearance was completed without other significant finds being made and it was now possible to make a detailed survey of what remained of the ship itself. Though the woodwork was represented only by a discoloration of the sand, the rusted nodules which contained the original clench-nails were all in position and from these the lines and dimensions of the ship could be taken with a high degree of accuracy. Added to this, a detailed photographic survey of every part was made by Miss Lack and Miss Wagstaff, so that all its features can still be studied at leisure. The last details were recorded, the last objects were removed and, on August 26, the excavation which had begun with Mr. Brown's first cutting on May 8, came to a close.

At this point we may review the problem of how the ship was transported from the river and placed in the grave-pit. Though the steep sandy scarp was a poor approach up which to drag so large a vessel, the northern fork of the small combe which runs down the scarp front near the ship-barrow would have provided a fairly simple approach. Between the two map-contours of 50 and 100 feet the horizontal distance is about 450 feet (140m) so that the gradient in this steepest part is about 1 in 9—the overall average being about 1 in 22—and, with the aid of the rollers, a strong party could have taken up the ship without undue difficulty. It is to be noted also that the barrow lies much closer to the head of the combe than does Barrow No. 2, where also a boat was buried. Now, as will later be seen, this smaller vessel was probably buried some thirty years before the great ship, so that the problem of its transport was still a living memory when the later burial had to be planned and doubtless due allowance was made for the larger vessel's much greater weight and bulk.

The second major problem was the placing of the ship in the pit. As will be seen from Fig. 6, it is certain that, though the grave was roughly shaped to fit the profile of the vessel, there was no long sloping ramp at the bow end, down which it could have been rolled.

There was only about $2\frac{1}{2}$ feet (75cm) between the sides of the pit and gunwales. Mr. Phillips accordingly formed the opinion that the ship must have been lowered horizontally into the pit. He had already noted a thin irregular layer of excavated sand on the old ground surface below the mound. From this he inferred that the pit was first excavated and the spoil cleared from the site, this thin layer being sand spilt during the removal. Then, he inferred, poles were placed across the trench and the ship was laid over its final resting place. By means of a line of bollards on either side, ropes were stretched across below the ship, enabling it first to be slightly raised while the poles were withdrawn and then to be gently lowered to the bottom of the pit. To this Mr. Phillips adds: 'No actual evidence for this method was found, but it is difficult to see how the operation could have been performed otherwise.'

Now this solution, though feasible enough, does present some difficulties. The width of the grave-pit was some 16 feet (4.8m) and the bollards, in order not to pull from the sandy matrix would have to be placed some distance from the pit's edge. The length of the rope between each pair of bollards would then be more than 20 feet (6m) and, when carrying the weight of the ship, would certainly sag considerably. Bollards would accordingly be needed which stood 4 or 5 feet (between 1.2–1.5m) above the surface and would therefore have to be buried to at least the same depth, as well as being very stout logs. It is possible, though perhaps unlikely, that such bollard-pits would not have been noticed in the ground in either the 1939 or 1967–70 excavations. Several ingenious solutions have been put forward to explain how the ship was put into the grave, but none are entirely satisfactory and the problem remains.

While these last stages of the excavation were progressing, other problems also exercised Mr. Phillips. The presence of gold and silver made necessary the holding of a coroner's inquest to decide the legal status of these pieces. Were they or were they not Treasure Trove? And so, on August 14 1939, the inquest was held to determine the answer to this question. Now the law of Treasure Trove is difficult and perhaps obscure. But without going into its history and merely outlining the modern practice in its interpretation, a simple summary may be attempted. All objects of gold and silver—and these metals only—when found, are to be promptly handed by the finder to the police. A coroner's inquest on them is then held and it is the duty of the jury under the coroner's direction to make a decision. If the objects were *hidden* in the earth or in some other hiding-place such as a cavity in a wall resting on the earth, *with the intention at the time of their being reclaimed*, then the objects still belong to the owner or his

51

legal heir. If the owner or his heir is unknown and cannot be ascertained, as must be the case when objects of antiquity are in question, the gold and silver are Treasure Trove and revert to the Crown. Where objects of archaeological interest are under consideration, the Crown is represented by the British Museum or its nominee—normally a suitable regional museum if the objects are not required for the national collection—and the antiquarian value is paid to the finder. The present purpose of this, of course, is not to confiscate for the financial value of the objects, but to preserve them where desirable for their scientific and artistic worth. If however the objects were 'dispersed', i.e. discarded or publicly disposed of with no intention of their being reclaimed, they are not Treasure Trove and so remain the property of landowner or finder according to the circumstances of their finding.

At this inquest it was made clear that the burial was a social function of its day, a religious ceremony carried out with a social sanction, when the grave-goods were placed in the grave in compliance with tradition. Some mention, it seems, was made of *Beowulf* and the funerals therein described. In fine, it was established that these grave-goods were *not hidden for safety* with any intention of their being reclaimed at a future date. The hoard therefore was adjudged not to be Treasure Trove and that, as landowner and finder—for she had initiated and controlled and, in its later stages authorised, the excavation for the purpose—they were the property of Mrs. Pretty.

And now followed an act of supreme generosity. The market value of the finds, not easily to be assessed, was vast. But Mrs. Pretty, realising that their true value lay in their unique archaeological importance, decided to forego any financial return for her efforts. On August 23, it was announced that the whole of the grave-goods of every kind had been given to the nation by Mrs. Pretty, as she deemed the British Museum to be the right and only suitable place for them to be housed. In this she was certainly right, but such insight and public spirit in the face of such great financial loss, are all too rare. And so the name of Edith May Pretty will always stand high in our list of national benefactors.

III

THE SHIP AND SOME OTHERS

THE CORRODING sand of the covering mound had not been kind to the fabric of the buried ship, for of its timbers there remained little more than a dark stain in the sand, with its ironwork a series of heavily-rusted nodules. But the skill of the excavators enabled the filling to be cleared without damage to these remnants of the vessel and it was possible to examine and record many of the details of its structure. For this difficult task, the excavators had the expert help of the late Lieutenant-Commander J. K. D. Hutchison, R.N., at that time on the staff of the Science Museum. In the first published description of the ship, given with Mr. Phillips' account of the excavation in 1940, insufficient allowance was made for the distortion brought about by pressure and suggestions were made about the stern of the vessel which are not tenable. But these in due course were corrected by R. C. Anderson and it is now possible to reconstruct this ship almost in its entirety.

To this end we are fortunate to have, in varying degree, detailed knowledge of other vessels of the same general type and period. From the East Anglian coast there are the smaller Sutton Hoo boat, the Snape boat and the Ashby Dell boat, all from sites in Suffolk. To these can be added the many boat-fragments from the Middle Saxon (i.e. c. A.D. 650–850) cemetery at Caister-on-Sea in Norfolk. But it is to the old continental home of the Angles that we must turn for the finest example for there, in the Schleswig-Holstein Museum of Prehistory, a complete ship of this type is still preserved. This ship, together with two others, was found lying in the peat of the Nydam Moss, Schleswig, in August 1863, when this province was still subject to the Danish crown. One was in parlous condition and could not be repaired; the second, built of fir, had to be left, but the third was duly extracted from its bed of peat. The Prusso-Danish war broke out,

Schleswig and Holstein were incorporated in the Prussian kingdom and the ship was removed to the Kiel Museum, where it was restored and preserved. Here it survived the bombing of the Second World War and was then taken to its present home. This ship, a rowing-galley dating from about A.D. 400, represents well the type used both by the first Anglo-Saxons in their attacks on the Roman province of Britain, and by their descendants of the true Settlement Period who came to Britain in the fifth and sixth centuries. More recently a somewhat similar vessel—as it was at first considered—was found near Utrecht in Holland and is there preserved in the Centraal Museum.

Though ancestral to the later Viking ships, these earlier vessels were much more primitive in design and construction and their seafaring qualities were correspondingly limited. Sidonius, a fifth-century noble-man of Roman Gaul, who wrote to a friend about the warfare of the Saxons, says: 'When you see the rowers of that nation . . .' and again, 'to these men a shipwreck is capital practice rather than an object of terror. The dangers of the deep are to them, not casual acquaintances, but intimate friends . . .' Historians have sometimes suggested that Sidonius exaggerated, but a study of these boats confirms that the risks of shipwreck must have been great.

Like the Viking ships, these Anglo-Saxon were clench- or clinker-built, i.e. with the lower edge of each plank overlapping slightly the upper edge of the plank below and riveted to it at frequent intervals by clench-nails of iron, clenched on the inside over an iron washer, the rove. This technique is still used in the building of most of our smaller boats, such as dinghies and longshore fishing vessels, though nowadays the fastenings are generally of copper. Ancient vessels of this build, however, can readily be distinguished from modern clinker-built boats by the method used to fasten the clenched 'skin' to the frames or ribs. In both ancient and modern vessels of this type, the lower part of the planking is clenched first and the ribs inserted afterwards. A modern vessel has the planking riveted directly to the ribs, but ancient builders had a different practice. As the planks were adzed—not sawn—from split tree-trunks, raised strips were left at suitable intervals and when the ribs were later inserted, these raised strips were shaped to fit them. Then, through holes bored in these cleats, as they are known, fastenings of bast, withies or tough roots were passed and lashed round the frames, a method used both in the earlier Anglo-Saxon and the later Viking vessels. It is claimed that this method of attachment gave great elasticity to the boat in a seaway. This is doubtless true, though with the wear and tear of rough usage, the lashings must frequently have parted and that in moments of stress.

It was, however, in the structure of the wooden 'skin' that great advances were made by Viking times. For the keel, Viking ships had a stout 'plank-on-edge', which gave great longitudinal strength to the vessel, whereas the earlier boats had no true keel of this type, but

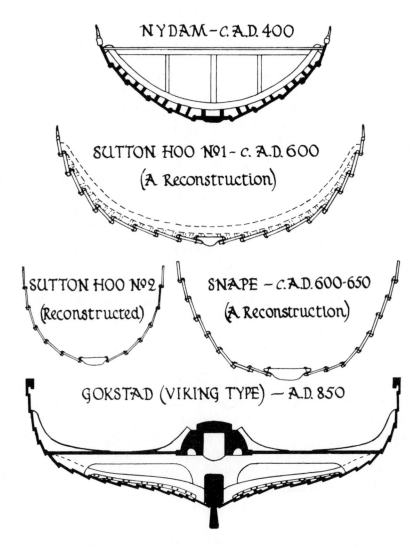

Fig. 10. Some midship cross-sections

55

merely a rather thicker plank than those adjoining it, set horizontally (Fig. 10). This gave a much less sturdy construction. Furthermore, the Viking shipwrights had learned to use narrow planks in comparatively short lengths, so that along the sides of the vessels there were frequent butt-joints where these short planks were pieced together. Each narrow plank carried only one cleat for attachment to each rib and the flexibility given by their use enabled well-rounded ships with high sheering ends to be built.

The earlier ships, however, were much simpler. That from Nydam was 73 feet 9 inches (22m) long overall. Each side was formed of six oak planks averaging 14 inches (35cm) wide—excluding the gunwale—and carrying two cleats for each rib. Except for the uppermost strake—i.e. a line of planking from stem to stern—each strake was made of a single plank. Even the uppermost—gunwale—planks were pieced only once on each side, in the bows of the ship. So comparatively intractable were these great planks that the vessel had a broad shallow flat-floored cross-section amidships and, towards each end, a narrow almost straight-sided V-shaped section. This, of course, gave a much less seaworthy craft than those of the Vikings and it is easy to see why 'shipwreck' was 'capital practice rather than an object of terror', for seafaring in the short steep seas of the shallow North Sea must indeed have been fraught with hazard.

There were other differences. The external plank-on-edge keel of the Vikings made it possible for them to sail their ships and, as is well known, their long passages were normally made under sail, with only occasional help from oars. But there is no evidence whatever that Anglo-Saxons of the Migration period had any sailing vessels at all. Certainly these flat-keeled ships would not have stood the strain of a single great sail. No trace of mast or rigging-fastening has been seen in any of those we know. And the reference by Sidonius to 'rowers' seems to confirm this conclusion.

The oblique evidence of contemporary literature also gives some confirmation. Bede in his *Ecclesiastical History*, includes a story told to him by Guthfrith, who later became abbot of Lindisfarne. Guthfrith and two of the brethren had gone by boat from Lindisfarne to Farne, some seven miles, to visit Ethelwald, the hermit successor of St. Cuthbert who died in 687. While returning to their own place, 'there ensued' in Guthfrith's own words, 'so great and dismal a tempest, that neither the sails nor oars were of any use to us, nor had we anything to expect but death'. By Ethelwald's prayers, however, the storm was stilled until they had reached land. Guthfrith then continues: 'When we landed, and had dragged upon the shore the small vessel that brought us, the storm . . . immediately returned.' Here there seems to be good evidence of a sailing-boat in approximately the last decade of the seventh century, though it is also clear that a boat 'dragged upon the shore' by three men cannot have been a seagoing clinker-built ship. There is a possibility, indeed, that this small vessel may have been a skin-covered curragh—the modern descendants of which may still be seen on the west coast of Ireland—but if so, it does not in any way help a discussion of clinker-built boats.

There is an Anglo-Saxon poem *Andreas*, in which the hero makes a voyage. In it we read that 'the candle of the sky grew dark, the winds rose, the waves dashed, the floods were fierce, the cordage creaked, the sails were soaked. The terror of the tempest rose up with the might of hosts; the thanes were afraid; none looked to reach land alive'. No longer, it seems was shipwreck a capital practice rather than an object of terror. This poem, of the so-called Cynewulf school, was not written before the second half of the eighth century and, more probably, may be dated after A.D.800. This seems to be almost the first certain reference to an Anglo-Saxon deep-sea sailing ship and is, of course, roughly contemporary with the opening of the Viking period, more than a century at least after the burial of the Sutton Hoo ship. The various references in the poem to 'the high-prowed vessel', 'the high-beaked vessel', also suggest a ship rather of Viking than of Nydam type.

There is one other reference which is somewhat earlier than the *Andreas*. This is in the epic poem *Beowulf*. In this poem, both the funeral ship of the mythical king, Scyld Scefing, and Beowulf's own ship which took him to and from the Danish kingdom, were sailing ships. But, though purporting to describe events which happened about the beginning of the sixth century, the poem in the form in which we have it was not composed until the eighth century and, with some degree of probability, near the middle of that century, if not a little later. We may, therefore, safely infer that it describes con-temporary ships and not those of the earlier period. This is confirmed by descriptions of the ship, e.g. 'the boat with twisted prow', 'the ring-prowed vessel', so reminiscent of the prow of the Viking ship from Oseberg (Pl. III). Again this gives a date at least a century after the date of the Sutton Hoo burial, thus tending to confirm that clinker-built sailing ships in Anglo-Saxon England began

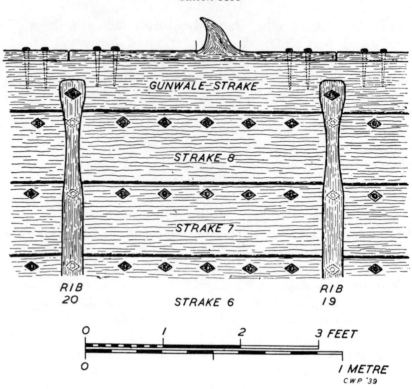

Fig. 11.　Suggested restoration of gunwale and upper strakes seen from the inside

first to make their appearance after A.D. 700, though small sailing-boats may perhaps have been in use from a slightly earlier date.

The inferred construction of the Sutton Hoo ship agrees generally, even closely, with that of the Nydam ship and the occasional differences arise from two centuries' more of experience in the shipwright's craft. Its overall length, as seen, was some 80 feet (24m), but as the uppermost part of both stempost and sternpost had been lost, it must originally have been 85 feet (26m), or even a little more. Its greatest beam was some 14 feet (4.2m) and its depth amidships 5 feet (1.5m). Its draught, when lightly laden, would have been some 2 feet (60 cm). Its keel appeared not to be of plank-on-edge type, but a horizontal plank of the Nydam type. This was probably rounded on its lower side, giving a slight external projection of some $2\frac{1}{2}$ inches (6cm) (Fig.10).

Of clinker build, it had nine planks a side, including the gunwale

58

plank. Amidships, these planks were about 15 inches (38cm) broad and were clenched at intervals of about 7 inches (17cm) , by clench-nails over diamond-shaped roves. It was noted that these roves were all carefully set so that their long axes were horizontal (Fig. 11). This would have required very careful workmanship in their setting and is perhaps rather unusual. The clench nails from the twelve boat-frag-ments at Caister all show, more or less, the line of the wood-grain in their rusty surface, and it is possible to say that these, which more probably belong to average boats of the period, are not set with any care as to their direction, though they have a similar diamond shape.

As this normal clenching continued under the ribs, it seems probable that these frames were fastened to cleats on the inner surface of the

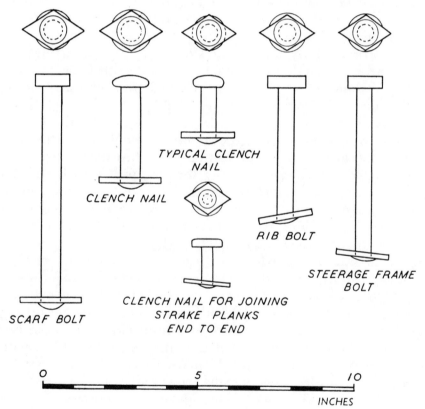

Fig. 12.   Various kinds of clench-nail used in the Sutton Hoo ship

planking, but this could not be confirmed with certainty. The stem and stern posts were joined to the keel with a scarf-joint, i.e. a long oblique half-joint, each joint being reinforced by three iron nails, $6\frac{1}{4}$ inches long (16cm), clenched over normal roves. Here there was a small variation from the Nydam pattern, for the latter ship had its fore and aft scarf-joints secured by the stout wooden pegs known as treenails. An added refinement lay in an iron strip nailed to the outer edge of the stern post, a protective device not seen in the Nydam ship. The planking details, however, were not those of Nydam, for each strake was built up of five lengths of plank, with the ends joined by short clench-nails, indicating the presence of half-joints giving flush surfaces.

In the Nydam ship, the 19 pairs of ribs were further secured by cross-braces or thwarts, resting on upright stanchions. To these thwarts were fastened the rowers' seats. The 26 pairs of ribs in the Sutton Hoo ship showed no evidence whatever of seats or thwarts, but these must have been cut away to accommodate the burial chamber. The Nydam ship was propelled by 15 oars a side and the oar-fittings on the gunwale are of great interest. Each oar was pulled against a single claw-shaped thole, to which it was attached by a grommet or ring of rope or hide. This passed through a hole in the base of the thole. These tholes were worked from naturally-grown forks, the longer arm of which was straight, with grooves cut to hold the lashings which fixed it to the gunwale. In the Sutton Hoo ship there were probably 19 tholes a side of similar shape, but the base pieces, each about 3 feet (1m) long, were attached to the gunwale by two or more iron spikes at each end. These ends were in contact with their neighbours and so formed a continuous rail around the gunwale. There was no evidence to show how the grommets were attached. (Fig. 17).

One structural puzzle which the excavators could not resolve was how the shipwright had attached the planking to the stem and stern posts. In the Nydam ship, a groove or rebate had been cut on each side of the posts into which the ends of the planks snugly fitted (Fig. 13). This may well have been done at Sutton Hoo, but is not certain. The remains rather suggested that this may have been done with the ends fastened in pairs by bolts which went right through both planks and the post. The shortness of bolts, however, rather tells against this interpretation. As will be seen below (p. 64), the strakes of the Snape boat were apparently fastened in this fashion.

The Nydam ship was steered by a large broad-bladed oar slung

60

(*a*).   Bronze bowls, angons and spearheads, when exposed.

(*b*).   The Nydam ship.

PLATE I

(*a*).   The Gokstad ship.

(*b*).   The Sutton Hoo ship: looking forward.

PLATE II

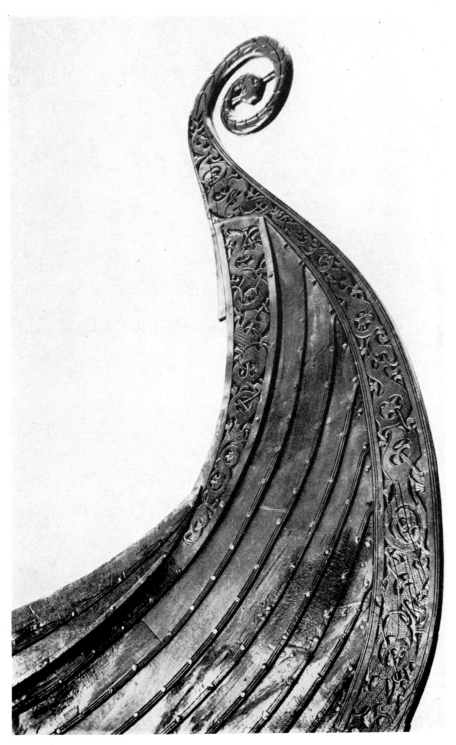

The Oseberg ship.

PLATE III

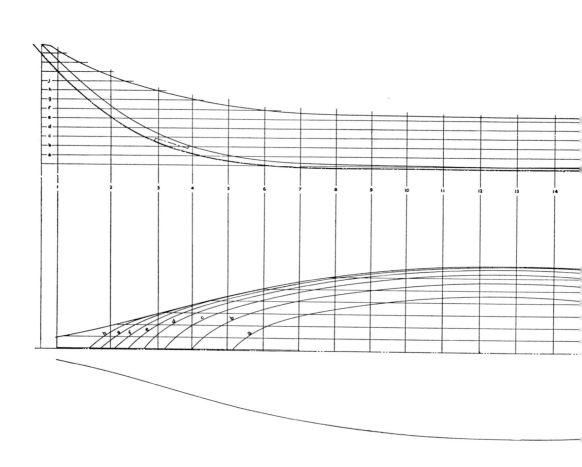

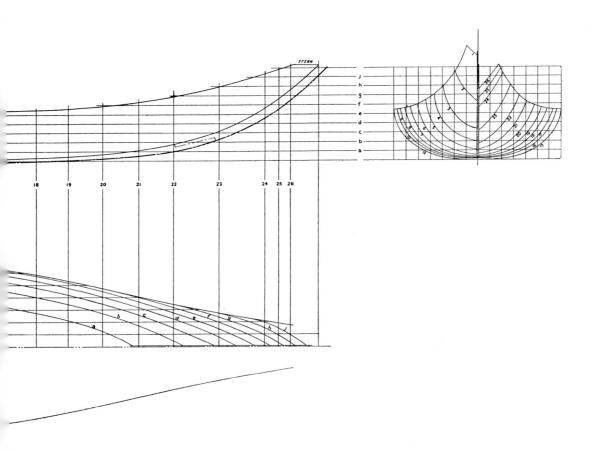

The lines of the Sutton Hoo ship.

PLATE IV

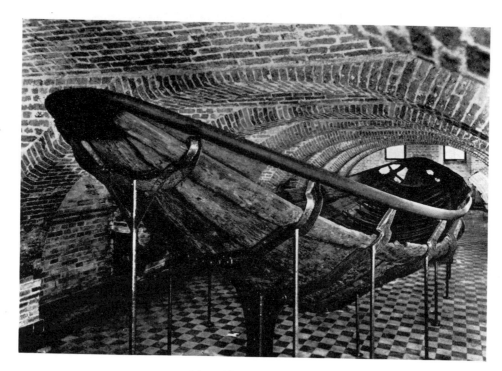

(*a*).   The Utrecht boat.

(*b*).   The Kvalsund boat.

PLATE V

(a).　The Sutton Hoo ceremonial whetstone.

(b).　The Hough-on-the-Hill whetstone.

PLATE VI

(*a*).   The bronze stag and iron ring from the top of the whetstone.

(*b*).   Panels (reconstructed) from the Sutton Hoo helmet.

PLATE VII

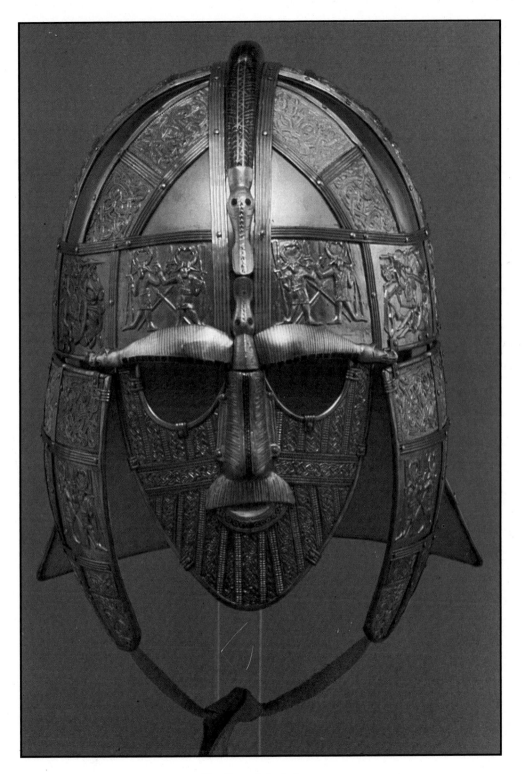

Replica of the helmet.

PLATE VIII

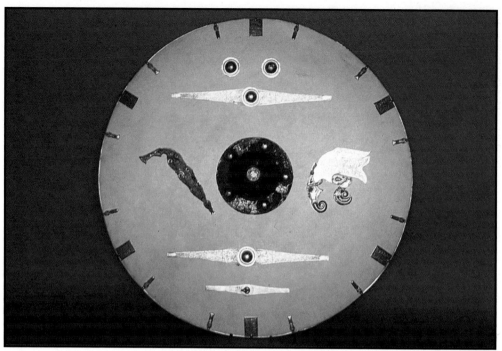

(*a*).   Reconstruction of the shield.

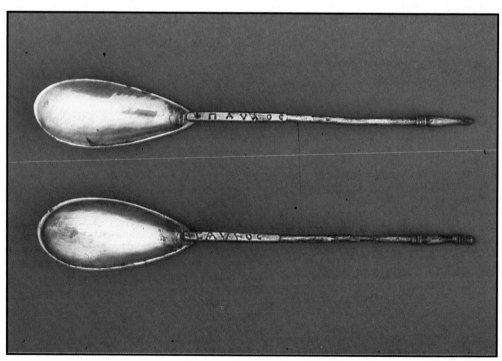

(*b*).   Inscribed silver spoons.

PLATE IX

(*a*).   Purse-lid.

(*b*).   Coptic bowl.

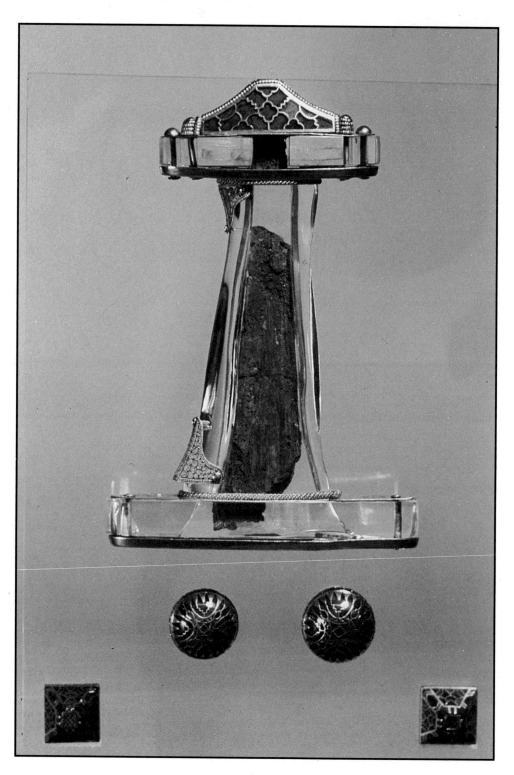

Sword, scabbard and baldric mounts assembled.

PLATE XI

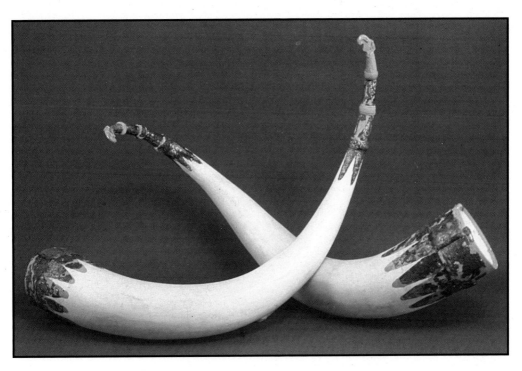

(*a*).   Two drinking horns with silver-gilt mounts.

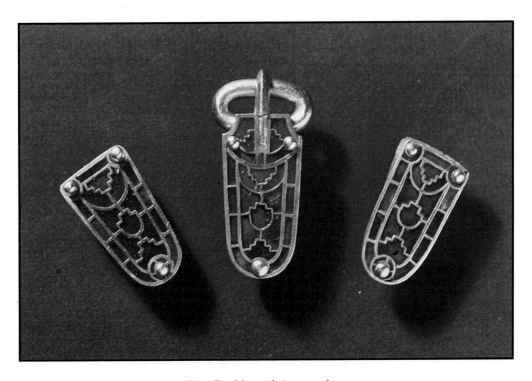

(*b*).   Buckle and strap-end set.

PLATE XII

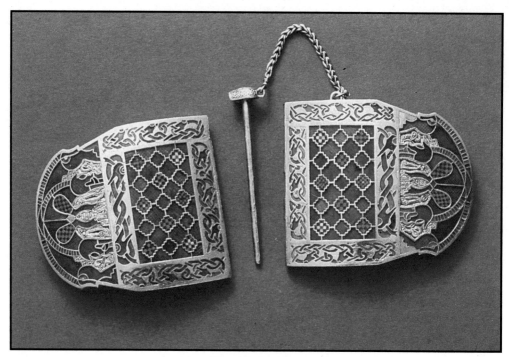

(*a*).   Hinged shoulder clasp.

(*b*).   The great gold buckle.

PLATE XIII

(*a*).   Byzantine silver bowls.

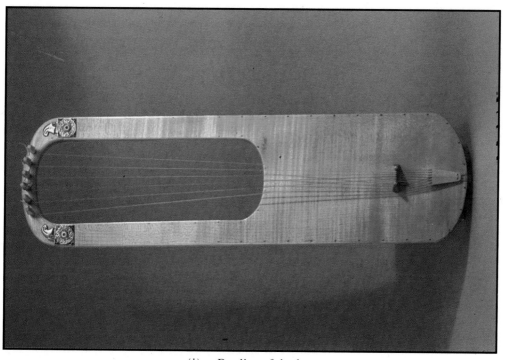

(*b*).   Replica of the lyre.

PLATE XIV

(*a*).   Celtic hanging-bowl.

(*b*).   Hanging bowl: side escutcheon.

PLATE XV

over the starboard quarter. At Sutton Hoo, no such steering-oar was seen, but the disposition of the ribs and their fastenings at this point, carefully designed to take the strain of the oar, showed that the steering mechanism was of Nydam type.

There was evidence that the Sutton Hoo ship was already old when it was buried. One seam amidships on the port side showed many additional clench-nails between the original ones. These had clearly been inserted in an attempt to tighten a strained and leaky joint. The stern scarf-joint, too, had been strengthened by additional nailing. Other slight abnormalities, however, probably belong to the deteriora-

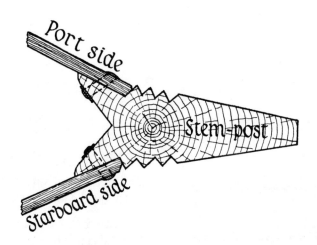

Fig. 13. Section of stem of Nydam ship showing method of attachment of strake ends

tion and decay undergone by the ship after it was buried. There was evidence that the gunwale lines, both fore and aft, had sprung away from the stem and stern posts. This had at first given rise to the suggestion that the ship had a narrow square or rounded counter-stern. Anderson showed that this shape would be assumed if the gunwale-ends had sprung from their fastenings and that, as would be expected, this ship was double-ended in the normal Northern fashion.

There had seemed at first to be some confirmatory evidence for this blunt-sterned variant in East Anglia. In Barrow No. 2 at Sutton Hoo, as has been described, a boat apparently about 18 feet (5.4m) long was found. In the absence of a competent boat specialist, this was less thoroughly surveyed and recorded than the great ship of 1939, but a plan was made by Mr. Brown, showing a boat with long pointed bow and a nearly square stern only a comparatively short distance aft of the greatest beam. From his notes made at the time, Mr. Maynard published a description of the constructional details of this stern, an article illustrated by sketches made by Mr. Spencer (Fig. 14). Careful study of this description makes it certain that this could not be a true stern at all, for it consisted only of short vertical boards held loosely

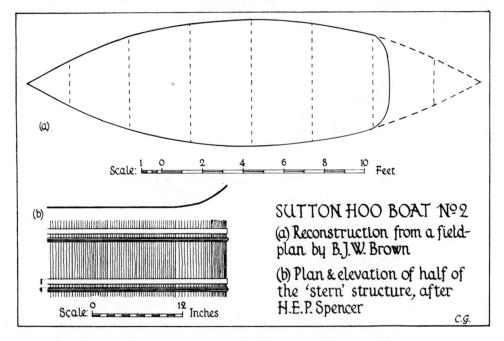

(a)

Scale: 1 0 2 4 6 8 10 Feet

(b)

Scale: 0 12 Inches

SUTTON HOO BOAT №2
(a) Reconstruction from a field-plan by B.J.W. Brown
(b) Plan & elevation of half of the 'stern' structure, after H.E.P. Spencer

C.G.

Fig. 14

together by iron strips without any nails, a quite impossible constructional method for a sea-going ship or, indeed, for any boat at all.

It will be remembered that the stern of this boat lay tightly against the end of the grave-pit, although the remainder of the boat had a gap of a foot all around. There were, too, on the original surface nearer the edge of the barrow, many loose clench-nails scattered around. It seems quite certain that one end of a normal double-ended boat—probably the stern, though this is by no means certain—was cut away and the larger portion was then lowered into the grave-trench.

The vertical boards were then inserted along a curved line to the very end of the trench to prevent collapse of the containing sand, and the iron bands bent round to hold them in position. The part which was cut away was probably burnt on the patch of red sand and the fallen clench-nails were the indestructible remnants from this fire.

When reconstructed, assuming that the curve of the sides was accurately recorded, the boat shows an approximate overall length of 22 feet 6 inches (6.85m), with a greatest beam of 6 feet (1.8m). The removed portion, therefore, must have measured more than 5 feet (1.5m) in length. The trench-profile was rather roughly recorded and shows a greater midship depth than would be expected. As however, this drawing showed a horizontal gunwale, there must be some error, as a complete absence of sheer is virtually impossible. It is more likely indeed that the stemhead and the gunwale near it were originally above the surface and a normal sheer took the gunwale below the trench-lip amidships. If so, the midship-section (see Fig. 10) is too deep by at least one strake. This reduction would give an internal depth amidships of about 3 feet (1m), a suitable dimension for a boat of this type and size.

It is possible to find some confirmation of this boat-cutting in the burials of seventh-century date found in the Middle Saxon cemetery at Caister. Here a number of graves were covered with sections, two, three or four strakes wide, cut from the sides of boats of from 20 to 40 feet long (6–12m). These were set longitudinally with the outer convex curve uppermost. But a single grave had the body laid *in* such a fragment, as was shown by the clench-nails being under the skeleton with the roves above the heads of the nails.

Yet another East Suffolk square-sterned boat of the same period has been published in the past and seemed to support the validity of the Sutton Hoo square stern. This lay below a burial barrow half a mile east of Snape church and was excavated in 1862. Three primary accounts of this excavation were published, each by a man who took some part in it, and each contributed something not noted by the others. With two of these accounts appeared a plan, longitudinal elevation and cross-section of the boat, the plan and cross-section purporting to show the disposition of the clench-nails. When found, these were merely rough nodules of rusted iron and the woodwork of the boat was little more than a stain in the sandy filling of the grave. Mr. Bruce-Mitford, however, has published an X-ray photograph of one of these rusty fragments and the original shape of the characteristic clench-nail can be clearly seen inside the rust.

The drawings show the boat to have had a flat floor which made a sharp angle with the outward-curving sides. It also had a broad, slightly rounded stern. The published plan, however, immediately raises doubt of its accuracy. Seventeen rows of clench-nails are shown, six rows on either side and five on the flat floor, one of them running along the keel-line in the middle of the floor. Furthermore, the second from the port side stops several feet short of the stern. Even more remarkable is the disposition of the clench-nails in the stern, for these are shown running right round the square stern in a quite impossible fashion. Of this plan Septimus Davidson, who was the leading excavator, says in a footnote: 'The plan, not having been made by a

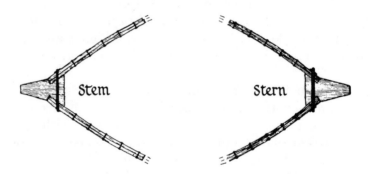

Fig. 15. Stem and stern fastenings of the Snape boat, reconstructed according to Davidson's description of the clench nails and end-bolts

professional surveyor, may not be minutely accurate, especially as to the exact position of the rivets at the smaller end.' To this we may add with confidence that they are even less accurate—as shown—at the larger end, for no boat could ever have satisfactorily been built in this fashion. And this is fully confirmed by Davidson's own written description, for of the clench-nails he says: 'The rows were six in number on either side and *four or five* [my italics here and below] in number at the bottom of the boat. At the sides the rivets lay horizontally, at the bottom they rested vertically on the sand. *All the rows terminated in two rivets lying parallel with each other—the one at the stem, the other at the stern.*' This can mean only one thing. The parallel bolts at stern held the ends of the two opposing strakes to the posts and this

64

implies that there *must* have been a sharp-ended stern comparable in shape with the bow. The explanation of this surprising error in the plan would seem to lie in the method of its preparation. The rough notes and sketch-plans would have been handed to the draughtsman to prepare the engraving for Davidson's published account. The draughtsman, knowing nothing of early 'Nordic' boats, doubtless strove to make the details fit the shape of the nineteenth-century clinker built transom-sterned boats he knew. And for a century his misconception has obscured the truth.

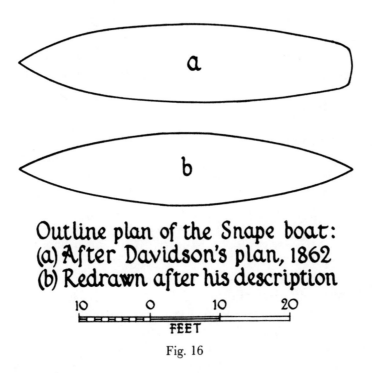

Outline plan of the Snape boat:
(a) After Davidson's plan, 1862
(b) Redrawn after his description

Fig. 16

Though the exact boat-shape shown in the cross-section is hardly credible as it stands, yet a reconstruction can be made (see Fig. 10). In this, the roves were carefully set on the recorded shape-line and the planking was restored, approximately as it must have lain, from these. It can thus be seen that this boat had not the broad shallow midship cross-section of either the Nydam or the Sutton Hoo ship (see Fig.10). Taken in conjunction with the other illustrations, it would appear to have been a boat designed for use in estuarine or inshore waters and not for open-sea crossings. The comparatively sharp angle between strakes 2 and 3—numbered from the keel—would lead to the roves being set obliquely to the head. A similar arrangement was noted in some of the Caister clench-nails which suggests that these, too, may have been inshore vessels of this pattern, a suggestion perhaps supported by the comparatively large number of different boats there recorded.

To complete the tale of these Anglo-Saxon boats from Suffolk, that found in 1830 in Ashby Dell, in Lothingland, must be described. It is probable that this boat was exposed during excavations for the planting of trees. A full record, together with drawings, was made by a Mr. Keable, estate carpenter, who was also described as 'agent and draughtsman to M. Mussenden Leathes of Herringfleet Hall'. An abstract of this record, by Keable's great-nephew, Kenneth Luck, was published in a local newspaper in 1927. Luck died in 1933 and his papers were burned by his landlady, so that there is little hope of learning more of this extraordinarily interesting boat. Though neither uncle nor nephew was versed in the detail of ancient ships, both were carpenters by training and so may reasonably be trusted to have given accurate descriptions of joints. This, as will be seen, is an important point when the details are assessed. Luck evidently regarded this as a Viking ship, as did many of those present when it was exposed. But in 1830 Keable had noted at the end of his description that 'Mr. Ruskin thinks the ship a Batavian and pre-Danish, the squire that she belonged to the Priory of St. Olaff [*sic*]'. Whoever Mr. Ruskin may have been, it is certain that he was close to the truth as the following description shows.

The dimensions of the Ashby boat are a a little difficult to understand. We are told that she was 54 feet (16.2m) long overall and 47 feet (14m) along the keel from stempost to sternpost, but that the upper parts of these posts had rotted away. As, however, the gunwale was present, very much cannot have been lost. If so, the boat cannot have had the long raking stem and stern seen in the Nydam and Sutton Hoo ships, but was in profile more like the smaller Sutton Hoo boat. On the other hand, the depth amidships was 6 feet (1.8m) and, from a line joining bow and stern, 9 feet (2.7m). There was, then, a 3-foot sheer, which is almost exactly that of the Nydam ship, though the actual hull-depth of the Ashby boat is greater.

The stempost was scarfed to the keel in normal fashion, but the sternpost was morticed to the keel, which would seem to imply that this post was straight and not curved. Both joints were secured by treenails. The shape of the keel's cross-section is not recorded, but we

66

are told that it was rebated to take the garboard—i.e., adjoining—strakes. This does not help in ascertaining the type of keel as, though rebating is essential with a plank-on-edge keel, both the Nydam and Sutton Hoo keels could be regarded as rebated by a man who did not understand their origin.

The planking is described as of 'riven larch . . . adzed . . . into form,' and each plank had two cleats for attachment to each frame. The cleats were slotted, with a hole on either side of the slot. The frames rested in these slots and were secured to the cleats by lashings passed through the holes. This is the technique employed in the

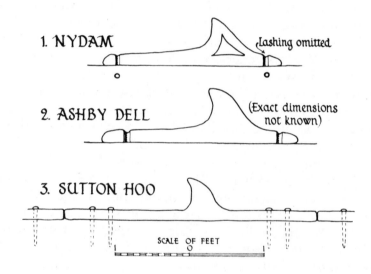

Fig. 17.   Some claw-shaped tholes

Nydam ship and the double cleats show that the planks were wide, in the earlier style. One difference, however, may be noted. The cleats were not carved from solid wood with the planks, but were made separately and affixed to the planks with treenails. The frames themselves were naturally-grown timbers and the cleats were 'eased or packed' where required to fit any irregularity.

The Nydam style is again seen in the tholes. These were claw-shaped, seven a side, and were lashed to the gunwale. Though there was provision for seven oarsmen only a side, there were fourteen thwarts with seats, fixed to the frames and gunwale plank with both treenails and lashings, though the detail of this is not given. And oars must have been the only method of propulsion, as there was neither mast-step in the keel nor any mast-seating in a thwart. From the stempost to the first thwart was a short cross-piece along the midship line and this held loosely a rounded timber, 9 inches (23cm) in diameter and 4 feet (1.2m) long. This had a horizontal hole bored right through it, apparently to take a small bar, and so led it to be regarded as a small capstan.

The most surprising feature of all appears to be that no iron was used in the boat's construction, all fastenings being either by treenails or by lashings through holes bored to receive them. If this is strictly true, the boat must have been clenched, not with iron rivets, but with lashings. Even this constructional method, primitive though it seems, is not without precedent for, in 1896, in a peat-moss at Halsnøy in Søndhordland, Norway, a boat clenched by just this method was found. It is described as generally of Nydam type, but with strakes still sewn by cords. It was dated to about A.D. 200 and was clearly an intermediate form between the ancestral elaborated canoe of Hjortspring type and the Nydam boat. There is evidence, also, that even as late as Viking times, some of the Nordland boats of North Norway were still sewn with sinews, at least in part.

The Hjortspring boat, found in the island of Als, Schleswig, in 1921, had a hull-length of 33 feet (10m) and a greatest width of 6 feet (1.8m). There was a single bottom plank, slightly concave amidships, the concavity tapering in long narrow grooves which ran out in 'rams' projecting beyond the hull. Each side was made of two broad planks lapped clinker-fashion, but sewn with bast and caulked with resin. There were raised cleats, three to a plank, in each of ten rows, to which frames were lashed with bast cords. As there was neither mast nor thole, she must have been propelled by paddling. This vessel, clearly developed from a dugout canoe by the addition of raised sides, was dated to about 300 B.C.

In assessing the true position of the Ashby boat in this sequence of vessels, one other factor must be considered. The boat was not lying in a silted-up gutter, but had been deliberately buried, away from any water-course. Though there is no record of any grave-goods or body in the ship, it seems that this may perhaps have been another of the Anglo-Saxon burial series.[1]

The Ashby boat, therefore, may be seen to possess somewhat discrepant features. The seams clenched by lashings and not by iron nails—for treenails will not satisfactorily serve for this—are a primitive feature. The lashed claw-shaped tholes and double cleats to a strake-width are in true Nydam style, as is also the oar-propulsion. The considerable sheer and the scarfed stempost are also true to the same style, but the morticed stern-post and the relative proportions of overall and keel lengths are not. They rather suggest a Roman influence. Here it may be noted, Ashby Dell lies only a few miles from Belton Fen which, lying in the shelter of the Saxon Shore fort at Burgh Castle, has elsewhere been suggested as the possible local head-quarters and dockyard of a detachment of the Roman fleet, the *Classis Britannica*, in the fourth century. If so, it is possible—and no more—that this boat was built for an early Anglo-Saxon settler before the last traces of Roman influence had disappeared. But, as is discussed below, boat-burial can hardly have been introduced before the early years of the seventh century, which weakens the possibility.

The keel, stempost and sternpost were said to be of elm, which is credible. But the planking of 'riven larch' seems to be impossible. Larch does not appear to have been available at this time, either in Denmark or England. It is probable therefore that the timber was from another coniferous tree and its species was mistaken by Keable.

The tale of early Anglo-Saxon boats is now almost complete. From Catfield, a village lying close to the Norfolk coast, comes the story of a 'Viking ship' found about 1855 in a sandpit in the middle of the village.[2] The sandpit site suggests that this may have been yet another ship-burial, but as no detail of the ship's type has survived, it cannot contribute to the discussion of early ships.

A few others of doubtful type are known but these, too, can contribute little to the discussion. At Walthamstow, Essex, a clinker-built vessel was found in 1830 while excavating the East London Company's reservoirs. It was clinker-built, some 20 feet (6m) long, and between the lapped planks was a caulking-pad of a 'cement in which cowhair was used'. This feature suggests a date for the boat as late at

[1] In 1956, Dr. J. M. Lambert and the writer made a series of borings around the approximate site of the boat in an attempt to determine if, indeed, it lay in the silt of a former creek. These borings showed no trace of open-water mud or estuarine clay, so that it must have been transported overland and buried.

[2] Information about this discovery was given to the writer by the son of a former rector. When a small boy, he heard the parish clerk report the discovery to his father, the rector.

least as the Viking period and, as other critical details are not recorded, it may here be disregarded.

In 1900, another clinker-built boat was found at Walthamstow. This, too, had some early-looking features, but as it was inverted over a burial of the Viking period and was clearly not a sea-going vessel, it may also be disregarded. Of another which still lies below King Street, Great Yarmouth, even less is known. That it had a pointed stem and was clinker-built with 2-inch (5cm) clench-nails was recorded when it was first exposed in 1886, and again about 1911. But from what is now known of the growth of the bank on which Yarmouth stands, it is reasonably certain that this ship cannot be earlier than the Viking period and may possibly postdate the Norman Conquest. Other early clinker-built vessels from Britain belong to the Viking period or a later day, and so need not be considered here.

The Utrecht boat, though when first found it was dated as second century A.D., may perhaps be likened to the second (1900) Walthamstow boat. It was found in 1930 in the sandy filling of an old channel of the river Vecht which, before about A.D. 860, was a main arm of the Rhine. Though primitive in some of its features and notably a flat keel-plank 47 feet (14m) long and 6 feet 7 inches (2m) broad amidships, it was certainly not a very early vessel (Pl. V (a)). A recent Carbon-14 test has given a date of A.D. 700 ± 100, which, though possibly a little in error due to the remains having been creosoted, appears to make it later in date than the Anglo-Saxon settlement period. This boat was clenched with iron nails in the forward part but aft with treenails, a construction very ill-suited to a sea going vessel. The method, however, is identical with that of the Walthamstow boat which also was clenched forward with iron and with treenails aft. The latter is generally regarded as a local river-barge used for the funeral of a Viking chief—to judge by his gold ornaments and sword—doubtless at a time when one of the party's own ships could ill be spared. There is some evidence that the Utrecht boat was fitted with a mast, though not in the normal Viking-ship fashion. Furthermore, double tholes for one pair only of oars were fitted and, as the boat is 54 feet 4 inches (16.5m) long and 13 feet 8 inches (4.2m) in beam, it is clear that it was not a normal rowing galley, but a river-craft of the eighth century or thereabouts.

From this survey, certain conclusions may be drawn. In spite of anomalous recording in the past, all early Northern clinker-built ships were double-ended and, before the end of the seventh century, on the English North Sea coast at least, were all oar-propelled. Of sailing ships in this period there is no real trace. Though the earlier Anglo-Saxon pirates must have been well-acquainted with Roman merchant vessels, which carried a large square sail and a small artemon, they did not themselves use such sails, probably because their craft lacked a strengthening plank-on-edge keel. This absence of sailing ships during the Settlement Period has, as is discussed below in Chapter VII, a very important bearing on the pattern of Anglo-Saxon settlement in eastern England, a bearing which justifies this somewhat close analysis, made possible by the discovery of the Sutton Hoo vessels. For this subject has not before been fully discussed and it will be seen not only to illuminate the origins of the 'Sutton Hoo group,' but also the whole of the Anglo-Saxon migrations.

It is true that, in the past, the Anglo-Saxons' possession of sailing ships has been suggested on the evidence provided by the Galtabäck ship, and this must now be examined. This ship was found wrecked on the west coast of Sweden, south of Varberg. With an overall length of 42 feet (12.6m) it was double-ended with flattish floor. It had an external plank-on-edge keel, to which the curved raking stem and stern posts were affixed by lapping joints which were not true scarfs. Its planks, ten strakes a side, were clenched, but were not attached to the frames by cleats and lashings, being clenched directly to the frames in more modern fashion. Furthermore, the frames were carefully-shaped timbers, not naturally-grown crooks and there was a carefully-constructed mast-step resting on the keel and a mast-seating in the afterpart of the appropriate thwart. Altogether the lines and structural detail are of a more modern type than either the earlier Migration or later Viking type of clinker-built vessel. By the analysis of the pollen-content of the containing peat-deposits, the Galtabäck ship has been attributed to the fourth or fifth century A.D., making it roughly of the same date as the Nydam ship. But this early date cannot be sustained for the lines, and particularly constructional details, make it impossible, there being too many anachronistic features. The true date is probably more nearly a thousand years later.

There remains one other vessel to be mentioned. The Kvalsund boat, the larger of two found at Kvalsund, Herøy, in Sunmøre, Norway, was excavated in 1920. It was characteristically double-ended, clinker-built, with its fine ends upturned in a fashion approaching that of the later Viking ships (Pl. V(b)). Its overall length was 59 feet (18m) and its beam almost 10 feet (3m). Its keel was a horizontally-set plank, but differed from the earlier keels by reason of a projecting rib which had been left along the centre-line of the outer side. The Norwegian ship-specialists, Dr. Brøgger and Professor Shetelig, considered this to be rather the first of the true Viking type than the last of the Migration type. Its rudder also was affixed to the boat's quarter in the more elaborate fashion, familiar from the Viking ships, required for a sailing vessel. This boat was tentatively dated by Professor Shetelig to about A.D. 600. But there is apparently no very cogent reason for so early a date and one at any time in the next century would seem to suit equally well. Even if the earlier date can be substantiated, this is after the close of the Anglo-Saxon Migration Period. In fine, with the Galtabäck ship discounted, there is no evidence whatever to suggest the presence of clinker-built sailing ships in England before the end of the seventh century and only the uncertain dating of the Kvalsund boat seems to preclude a similar statement for the Scandinavian North.

As a result of the 1966/67 excavations, specialists were able to make a new study of the remains and consequently the description of the boat requires alteration in a number of details. Its original length had been 89 feet (27m)— some 4 feet (1.2m) longer than the original estimated–and 4 feet 6 inches (1.37m) deep, rather than 5 feet (1.5m). It was thought that there had been benching for forty rowers rather than the thirty-eight suggested by Mr. Phillips. The absence of tholes, the spikes against which oarsmen pulled their oars, in the midships area had been noted by the original excavators. It was thought that these had been removed when the burial chamber was constructed. However, comparison with the boat excavated at Graveney in Kent in 1970 raises again the possibility that a mast with a large square sail had been set amidships. The Graveney boat, though later in date (c. A.D. 950) than Sutton Hoo, had a similar keel-plank and is likely to have been a sailing vessel. Some specialists now consider that, structurally, there is no reason why the Sutton Hoo boat should not have sailed, but no evidence was recovered.

B. G.

IV

THE GRAVE-GOODS: 1

THE GRAVE-GOODS had been laid out in the burial chamber roughly in the shape of an H. The more important and ceremonial objects lay along the west end of the chamber and the keel line. Along the east wall lay the domestic objects.

Along the western wall lay the iron stand. In the 1940 report of the excavation it was shown on the plan as 'lamp stand' and, in the text, was called 'the flambeau'. It was described as an iron bar 5 feet 3 inches (1.6m) long with the lower end spiked and the upper end carrying an equal-armed cross set horizontally, the four arm-ends each carrying a stylised bull's head ornament. Eleven inches (28cm) below this was another horizontal fitting, a square gridded frame, also decorated at each corner with a similar bull's head. From these there had apparently once been thin stays running downward to a more closely-set third bracket on the rod though, when found, these stays had been largely destroyed by rust (Fig. 18). It could be carried, its estimated weight originally being 11 lb 10 oz (5.3kg); the spiked end suggests that it was intended to be stuck into the ground or into a socket. Nothing quite like it has been found before in Britain or on the Continent. Some people believe it is a lamp while others think it is a standard; its position at the west end of the chamber suggests it probably had some ceremonial function. This will be discussed later in Chapter VI. It is quite likely that the stand had been placed upright in the chamber, perhaps propped against the end wall, and when the chamber collapsed, the stand fell over damaging some of the other objects at this end.

Closely associated with the standard was the decorated stone bar. It has been called a whetstone, but has never been used for sharpening any blade, nor is it a suitable implement for sharpening a sword. The bar, which is just under two feet long (58cm), has a square cross-

73

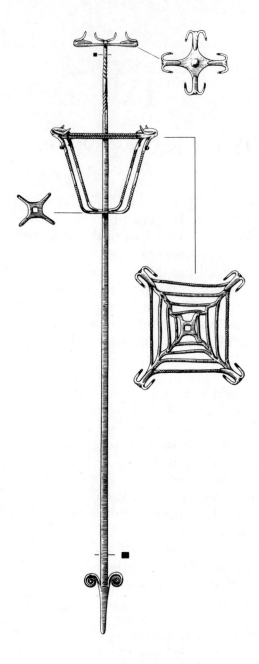

Fig. 18.   The iron standard

section and is slightly tapered towards each end, the ends themselves being carved into a slightly lobed, nearly globular shape, which had once been painted red. Each face of both tapered ends bears a stylised face carved in relief and set in a pear-shaped frame; three of the faces are bearded. It is possible that all the heads at the top are women's while those at the bottom are men's. Attached to one end by an openwork cage of thin bronze strips was a shallow bronze saucer, while at the other end, also attached by bronze strips, was an iron ring surmounted by a bronze stag. For many years it was thought that this belonged to the iron stand, but recent work in the British Museum has shown otherwise. The bronze stag is unlike any other piece from the burial group and it has been suggested it is an old piece, perhaps from the fifth or sixth century, re-used on the sceptre.

Stone bars decorated usually with a single head have been found in Ireland, Wales, and particularly Scotland. A fragment of another was discovered at Hough-on-the-Hill, in Lincolnshire, though not in the pagan Saxon cemetery in that parish. In 1868 a four-sided stone bar, decorated at the end of one face with three grooves, was found standing upright at the foot of a burial at Ulceby in Yorkshire. The stone from which this bar was made was very similar to the stone of the Hough and Sutton Hoo examples. The stone can be closely matched by rocks in the Southern Uplands of Scotland and north-west England. But blocks of this stone have been found in eastern England, moved there by glaciers during the Ice Age. This amazing piece therefore has affinities with Celtic Britain in the West and North. But though the form of this stone bar can be paralleled satisfactorily only in Britain, the style and type of faces belong elsewhere. Similar faces are to be found on the Sutton Hoo shield itself, while others are found particularly in Scandinavia. Dr. Bruce-Mitford has suggested that this strange ceremonial object was a sceptre and was made in the royal workshops in south Suffolk. It will be further discussed in Chapter VI.

Near the standard and sceptre were the remains of a shield. Its wooden body had long since been reduced by decay, but the metal fittings and other embellishments were sufficiently intact to be treated and restored; they have enabled the whole shield to be reconstructed. When this was done, the shield was seen to be circular, about 36 inches (91cm) in diameter and slightly dished on the inner side. The body of the shield was of wood, about 5/16 inch (7mm) thick, protected on both sides by a thin covering of leather. The edge was protected by a U-section binding of bronze gilt. It was held in place by six (perhaps originally twelve) rectangular panels of gold foil and twelve dragon heads in gilt bronze, set radially.

The great shield boss, which covered the central hole where the back of the hand lay, is of iron, variously decorated with gilt-bronze, niello-inlay and garnets; some of this metal bears the form of dragon heads and other parts carry zoomorphic designs. This boss was held in position by five domed rivets. The iron hand grip, about $4\frac{1}{2}$ inches (12cm) long, crossed the opening in the shield covered by the boss; it was slightly off-centre so that there was room for the knuckles and back of the hand within the hollow boss. The grip was extended above and below the boss by two decorated iron bars covered with gilt-bronze. These extensions were held by rivets with domed heads on the front of the shield, each in the centre of a long tapering gold panel. Set above the upper domed rivet were two more domed rivet-heads. These rivets passed through the shield to hold a horizontal strap at the back which was probably used to hang the shield up when not in use. This was quite separate from the carrying strap which was held by a loop at one end round the grip and anchored to the board at the other above the hanging strap. On either side of the boss were a winged dragon and a stylised bird. The dragon is of gilt bronze with relief-decoration, further embellished with tinning, niello-work and garnet-inlay. The bird has a gilt-bronze head inlaid with garnet, and a projecting crest in the form of another bird or dragon's head. The leg is of gilt and tinned bronze with, at the hip, a pear-shaped area containing garnet inlay within which is a human face, reminiscent of some on the sceptre. The bird's wing and bifid tail are of wood covered with decorated gold foil, while the body, of which only traces remain, has been conjecturally restored. The final piece of decoration on the front of the shield, set below the lower dome-headed rivet holding the grip extension, is a gilt-bronze 'ring' found in a lump of sand in the British Museum Laboratory. Such 'rings' are normally found attached to pommels of swords. They differ from the Sutton Hoo 'ring' in that the lower lobe is usually cut at an angle to fit the slope of the pommel. The only other known example of a sword-ring which has not been cut at an angle is one from a Swedish boat-grave, Valsgärde No. 7. Here the ring was mounted on a drinking horn. Certain features on the Sutton Hoo ring have closer affinity with those of East Scandinavian sword-rings than English rings.

Other features of the Sutton Hoo shield invite close comparison with Scandinavian shields. Shields from Swedish graves at Vendel and

Valsgärde were decorated with birds and dragons and at Vendel too, the bird on the shield from Vendel I has only head and leg made of solid metal as at Sutton Hoo and indeed, the whole design of the bird is East Scandinavian. It has been suggested that the same man made the dies used to stamp decoration on the long tapering gold strips which decorate the Sutton Hoo shield and one from the Vendel 12 grave. Despite these and other points of similarity with Scandinavian shields, there are some important points of difference, for instance the Sutton Hoo shield is probably made from lime wood while the Scandinavian shields are of pine. Dr. Bruce-Mitford has therefore suggested that the shield was made in East Anglia by a Swedish craftsman.

A 'Swedish connection' is suggested too, by the helmet, the remains of which were found lying to the east of the shield. In 1947, Mr. Maryon of the British Museum Laboratory wrote:

'When unpacked . . . the remains . . . covered a good-sized table. They appeared to consist of a gilded bronze nose and mouth piece, two gilded bronze dragon heads, parts of what once had been a silver crest, and three or four hundred fragments of sand-encrusted rusty iron . . . Though almost all of the pieces were of iron they were so corroded that little metal remained . . . Some were friable; others had become mineralized and, in fact, had been partially transformed into limonite—a hydrate of iron. Traces of ornament and mouldings showed upon them.'

Doubts were expressed about some of the elements of the helmet and a new reconstruction was made 1970–71 by Mr. Nigel Williams, a Conservation Officer in the British Museum.

The helmet was basically a hemispherical iron cap to which were attached vizor, cheek-pieces and a neck guard of iron. The vizor was rigidly secured to the cap but the cheek-pieces and neck guard were hinged with leather. The neck-guard movement was minimal but the cheek pieces could be pulled close to the face and fastened with tapes beneath the chin. The cap, which was lined with leather, was large and there was space inside for padding. The wearer could adjust the amount of padding to fit the head. The head was further protected from weapon-blows by the tubular crest which ran from back to front. This was an iron tube encased in silver of about $\frac{1}{8}$-inch (3mm) thickness and its ends carried gilt-bronze dragon heads. Other bronze fittings are the eyebrows, further decorated with silver wire and niello-inlay and edged below with garnets inset over gold foil. The eyebrows are further embellished with a gilt boar's head at each outer end. A single bronze casting also comprises the nose and mouth-piece of the vizor, again decorated with silver and niello-inlay.

The nose formed the body and the eyebrows the outstretched wings of a dragon whose head filled the space between the eyebrows and whose snout met the snout of the dragon's head at the front of the crest. To complete the adornment, the iron surfaces of the cap and its attachments were originally covered with very thin sheets of tinned bronze decorated with panels in relief and further bound at the helmet-edges by a rim of gilded bronze. Though the helmet looks dull enough to us after centuries of change and decay, how right was Mr. Maryon when he said: ' . . . we have to imagine it in its original condition as an object of burnished silvery metal, set in a trellis-work of gold, surmounted by a crest of massive silver, and embellished with gilded ornaments, garnets and niello—in its way a magnificent thing and one of the outstanding masterpieces of barbaric art'.

Some idea of this is given by the replica made at the Tower Armouries. On this the decoration has been restored. The panels of relief-decoration fall into five groups. Two of these are varieties of interlace-ornament and three contain figure-groups. Of these, one bears a mounted warrior overriding a fallen foe, another has a pair of standing warriors, each with a crescentic-winged helmet; of the third practically nothing can be ascertained. The designs of these figure-groups are familiar from Swedish examples and confirm the close resemblance of this helmet to several found in seventh-century burials in the Uppland province of Sweden, though the Sutton Hoo specimen appears to be a finer and more elaborate example than those of the Swedish graves. This helmet was not new when it was buried and there are some hints that it had been repaired.

Other items lying at the west end of the chamber associated with a warrior were the iron heads of five spears and three barbed throwing spears or angons. About 7 feet (2.2m) to the east lay the iron ferrules from the ends of the wooden shafts of the angons. A sixth spearhead, originally identified as a scramasax lay parallel with the sword. There must have been some reason for its isolation from the rest; perhaps it was the favourite spear of the man buried here.

Three of the angon heads were thrust through one of the two looped drop-handles of a bronze Coptic bowl. Standing bowls of this type, though not very common, are well-enough known in a pagan Anglo-Saxon setting; at least six other examples have been recorded from Suffolk and Norfolk. These bowls are imports and derive originally from the Near East. It is thought that this example may have come from Alexandria. The Sutton Hoo bowl differs from others found in England by having a solid foot-stand and a line of animals engraved inside the bowl. They have been identified as a camel, a donkey, a lion and another large feline, perhaps a tiger.

Wedged inside the Coptic bowl was another bronze vessel of a type known as a hanging bowl. This may well originally have been hanging on the west wall of the chamber, because an iron nail was found rusted to a suspension ring. Nearly a hundred of these bowls—some only in fragmentary form—are known and they pose one of the problems, still unsolved, of early Anglo-Saxon archaeology. In essentials, the Sutton Hoo bowl is typical of the series, but the quality and kind of its embellishments make it an outstanding piece. These hanging-bowls have rounded bases and loop handles designed for suspension. The loop handles are secured to the body of the bowl by hooks which are themselves appendages of broad medallions known as 'escutcheons'. The escutcheons are frequently decorated with enamel in the curvilinear patterns which characterise Late Celtic art; but it is a late phase of this art which not uncommonly shows the influence of Romano-British styles of decoration. The Sutton Hoo bowl has three such round escutcheons holding its suspension-hooks. Beneath each of these escutcheons is a casting in the form of a boar's head with garnet eyes. The three intermediate spaces each hold a rectangular escutcheon—a less usual feature—and another round medallion or 'print' on the outside of the convex base. Finally, on the inside of the bowl, set on a stem springing from yet another round escutcheon, is a bronze fish decorated with enamel. This fish has been identified as a rainbow trout.

All the escutcheons on this bowl are richly enamelled and further decorated with millefiori glass fragments in the enamel. Millefiori glass originated in the Near East and is made by fusing together into a thicker single rod many thin rods of different colours. The thick rod is then cut across into thin slices, each of which shows a mosaic of the original colours. Another interesting feature of the bowl lay in its having been repaired; its surface showed several small silver patches riveted over holes in the original bronze. The largest of these patches is decorated internally with zoomorphic ornament similar to that on other pieces in the hoard; the repairs, it is clear, were carried out by an East Anglian goldsmith.

When found under controlled conditions and their associations made clear, these bowls are customarily seen to have been buried in pagan Anglo-Saxon graves. On occasion, indeed, they have occurred in use as cremation urns holding calcined bone fragments. Sometimes detached escutcheons only are noted and an escutcheon has been seen worn as a trinket.

Many of the techniques and details are clearly derived from Romano-British sources, such as the spots of enamel on the body of the fish in the Sutton Hoo bowl. There must have been a number of workshops producing these hanging-bowls in Scotland and perhaps in Wales and Northern England.

In the Coptic and hanging bowls lay fragments of another object of outstanding interest, a musical instrument. This was a lyre, a six-stringed instrument about 29 inches (74cms) long made of maple-wood. Originally it was reconstructed as a harp, but a careful re-examination of the surviving fragments of wood showed that it had originally been an oval, symmetrical instrument. These lyres are known from graves on the continent and in England and from manuscript illustrations. The strings, probably of gut, were fastened at the sound-box end to a tailpiece and stretched across a bridge to wooden pegs projecting through holes in the top of the instrument. These pegs could be turned to tune the strings. The lyre had been buried in a beaver-skin bag and probably hung from the chamber roof. It fell across the Coptic bowl and broke. The whole of the lower part of the instrument, that is the sound-box and its fittings, had decayed away. Missing too, were fittings for the short strap which the player twisted round his left wrist and which helped to steady the instrument while it was being played. Evidence for the existence of these straps, known from manuscript illustrations, was found on the Bergh Apton, Norfolk lyre discovered in 1973.

A few other items were found in the complex along the west wall. A small bronze bell, perhaps imported from the East Mediterranean, lay between the sceptre and the shield. Also from the shield area were the fragmentary remains of four or five ivory gaming pieces. From the number of gaming pieces found in Anglo-Saxon graves, board games were a favourite pastime of the period. Near the top of the iron stand were the iron fittings of a wooden bucket which had originally been about 14 inches (35cms) high. As another bucket and containers of a type normally found in a kitchen stood at the other end of the chamber, this bucket must have contained something very special.

To the east of the bucket lay a stack of eight silver bowls lying upside down. Two others had slipped sideways off the stack and partly covered two silver spoons. Three of the bowls were badly decayed. The bowls were all between 8 and 9 inches in diameter (20–23cms) and with rounded bases. Each is decorated with a formalised geometric leaf design set in a roundel which forms the centre of a four-armed cross; the arms of the cross extend to the rim of the bowl. Eight of the bowls make up four pairs, but the designs on the other two are different. These bowls were made by Byzantine craftsmen, probably in a single workshop about A.D. 600, in Eastern Europe or the Near East. The best parallels are the bowls found in Turkey in the Lampsacus treasure. Dr. Bruce-Mitford has suggested that these bowls may have a Christian significance.

From this same Lampsacus treasure come the best parallels for the spoons. These belong to a well-known type with fig-shaped bowls and simple, slightly balustered stems. They have been two of the most debated items in the hoard. Each bears a simple inscription in Greek letters, on one the name SAULOS and on the other PAULOS. These spoons are regarded by some as a pair of Christening spoons, presented to a convert at his baptism, so that they hold a significant place in the discussion of the subject of the burial. The spoons were not inscribed by the same craftsman. The Paulos inscription was engraved by a craftsman used to working on spoons. The other inscription was produced by an engraver who may well have been a cutter of coin dies and unfamiliar with Greek. It may not have been meant as Saulos but was an inept copy of Paulos. It has been suggested that the inscription was added at a Merovingian mint to provide a pair of inscribed spoons.

Immediately to the east of the bowls, near the keel-line, lay the sword and the gold jewellery. The discussion of these items will be left to the next chapter.

On the keel-line, in the centre of the deposit, were the remains of eight drinking vessels which had been covered with cloth. Little survived beyond the silver-gilt decorative mounts. Two of the vessels were a pair of bull's horns of the great wild ox, the aurochs (*Bos primigenius*), known to us in Julius Caesar's writings as the Urus. Measured along the curve these horns were about 3 foot long (90cms) and each held about 3½ pints (2 litres). Such horns were used for drinking ale or mead in the king's hall and were passed from hand to hand. The aurochs was extinct in Britain well before the Roman period but continued to live in the forests of central Europe, the last known of these animals being killed near Warsaw in 1627. These two Sutton Hoo horns, therefore, must have been brought to East Anglia, probably from the North German Forest.

The other drinking vessels, originally thought to be horns, are now known to be wooden bottles, each hollowed out of a single piece of maplewood. Although there is no direct evidence for the form of the bottles, it is thought that they had globular bodies with cylindrical necks, and probably with flat bases so they could be set on a table.

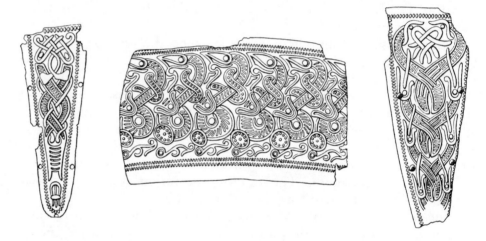

Fig. 19.   Designs from silver mounts of drinking horns (about I/I)

Wooden drinking vessels are known from a number of Anglo-Saxon graves.

Both the drinking horns and the bottles had similar mounts. Around the mouths were rectangular panels, below which were a series of triangular panels all stamped with animal ornament. Only two dies were used for the mounts around the mouths of the horns; different decoration embellished the mounts around the pointed end of the horn which ended in a bird's head terminal. Two different dies were used to stamp the mounts on the wooden bottles. Covering the drinking vessels were the remains of textiles and leather. These represent perhaps a leather tunic, a cloak or blanket, some wall hangings and other garments, all carefully folded before being placed over the drinking vessels. Evidence for textiles was found throughout the burial, almost always with metal, for in most cases the fibres had been mineralised (replaced with metallic oxides) as the result of the corrosion of bronze and iron. But gold does not corrode so no textiles were preserved in this area.

Some way from the drinking vessels, at the southern edge of the burial deposit, were the iron hoops and handle of a wooden bucket, probably made of yew.

Next to the drinking vessels, along the keel line, lay an amazing complex of objects covered by a large silver dish. This circular salver, some 2 feet 3 inches (69cm) in diameter, has a slightly raised rim and a deep footstand. It is ornamented with engraved classical designs and, on its base, there is the equivalent of our modern hall-mark, four impressed stamps which are the imperial assay marks of the Byzantine (Eastern Roman) Empire. They are those of the Emperor Anastasius I, who reigned from A.D. 491 to 518, during which time this dish was tested and stamped. The survival of this dish for a century and a half before being buried is a pointer to the difficulty of dating a burial with precision by one item of its grave-furniture, unless corroborated by other evidence such as was found here. It shows, also, how wide was the field from which this East Anglian treasure was drawn.

Pinched onto the foot-ring of this great dish was the cup of a silver ladle. When the roof of the burial chamber collapsed, the impact damaged and distorted a number of objects and pushed the foot-ring of the dish into the ladle which had been lying beneath it. The ladle handle was found detached, lying in a silver bowl which lay partly hidden beneath the great silver dish. This bowl, also distorted by the impact of the collapsing roof, is about 16 inches (40cm) in diameter, with internally fluted sides. On the inside of the base, within a band of formal design, there is a medallion with a crudely-executed classical female head in low relief. The dish also has a pair of drop handles. It is difficult to date, but is perhaps most likely to be the product of some East Mediterranean workshop in the sixth or even very early seventh century. Besides the ladle handle, the bowl contained a small plain silver bowl and eight small walnut burrwood bottles. A burr is an outgrowth on a tree, the wood of which is softer than normal, and is therefore very suitable for making small pots. These bottles were similar in shape to small squat Anglo-Saxon glass bottles found, for instance, at Faversham in Kent. They had silver gilt metal strips around the mouths, held in position by metal clips, which also held sheet-metal zoomorphic panels. The decoration of these bottles is very similar to that on the drinking horns and cups. It is thought that these bottles were probably used to contain some ointment or salve.

Also inside the fluted bowl was a wooden object, perhaps a box, some iron escutcheons, three bone combs and four iron knives with horn handles and the possible remains of their leather sheaths.

Beneath the fluted bowl was a mass of iron mail. It was badly rusted and cannot be unwrapped. It is probably a knee-length coat of mail which had been neatly folded when it was put in the burial chamber. Mail coats have been found in boat burials at Vendel and Valsgärde. Figures wearing knee-length mail coats with short sleeves are shown on, for instance, a helmet from Vendel and on the Franks casket probably made in Northumbria about 700. The Sutton Hoo coat was made of alternate rows of welded or forged links and of riveted links. Near to the chain mail was an iron axe-hammer. The long iron handle had been made separately from the iron head and then forged to it. A fitting at the end of the handle was perhaps of a ring. This is likely to be a war-hammer.

Beneath the great silver dish were two bronze hanging bowls, both upside down. The decoration on the three enamelled hook escutcheons on the smaller bowl is Celtic, similar to that found on Irish and North British bowls. The second bowl is quite different from this and from the hanging bowl found at the west end of the burial chamber. It shows a mixture of Germanic and Celtic decorative techniques and designs. It has circular hook escutcheons cast in one piece and originally covered with stamped foil in the Germanic manner, while the large circular basal escutcheons have zoomorphic swastika designs against red enamel. This bowl is not likely to have been made in a North British workshop. It has been suggested that it is the result of collaboration by two workmen, one trained in a Celtic workshop and the other by a Germanic metalsmith. Beneath this hanging bowl was a horn cup and nearby was a maple wood bowl or scoop. From beneath the great silver dish came a single gaming piece, probably of ivory and similar to those found at the east end of the chamber.

Little mention has yet been made of the mass of leather and textile which forms part of this complex. The foot ring of the silver Anastatius dish was sunk in a mass of goose down and textile. The down is from a pillow with linen and perhaps woollen covers. Remains of feather pillows or bedding have been found from other cemeteries and there was the possibility of a similar pillow in mound 4 at Sutton Hoo. It is impossible to be certain what objects are represented by all the pieces of textile and leather, but they include perhaps a leather tunic, a cloak and a pair of trousers and the remains of at least two pairs of shoes associated with tapes and decorative braid. These latter are high class light weight shoes perhaps made for indoor wear. One of the soles may be an inner sole or shoe sock. One of the shoes was English size 7. From in or beside the fluted silver dish came the remains of a woollen cap edged with otter fur. In addition to the textiles were a number of small bronze and silver buckles and strap ends which may come from these or other unrecognised garments. The whole pile of objects, with the probable exception of the Anastasius dish, was covered with a large cloth, perhaps a cloak.

The excavators recorded that this complex lay on a wood tray such as was found at Barrow No. 3. But nothing now survives and the wood may have been part of the burial chamber floor. Near to the complex, but not part of it, was a pottery bottle, while just to the east of this lay an iron lamp. The hemispherical bowl, supported on three legs, contained a cake of beeswax. A similar lamp was found in a burial at Broomfield in Essex.

Beyond this lamp, and lying in a line along the east wall of the burial chamber, were a group of large domestic containers and a mass of chain work. At the northern end were the metal fittings of a great wooden tub. It was made of yew wood staves held in position by an iron rim and hoops probably around the middle and just above the base. It stood on iron feet, and it had two loop handles and decorative fittings. The tub probably contained about a hundred litres (22 gallons). Large tubs have been found in other English burials and in Scandinavian ship burials. When found in ships they have been interpreted as water containers, and this may well be the case at Sutton Hoo.

Remains of the iron fittings of a third iron bucket were found inside the tub. Such iron bound buckets and tubs are not found in Germanic graves in England before the sixth century.

Partly covering the tub and bucket were the shattered remains of a large sheet-bronze cauldron. To the south of this lay the remains of two smaller cauldrons, also of sheet-bronze and each with two pierced vertical lugs to take an iron handle. These belong to a well-known type, found in a number of Anglo-Saxon cemeteries. The large cauldron was somewhat different, having a pair of iron rings for suspension. It had possibly been hung by one of these handles from a nail fixed into the wall of the burial chamber. A very similar cauldron was found in the rich Taplow burial.

Associated with the large cauldron was a mass of rusted ironwork. During the war it disintegrated and the reconstruction of the elaborate suspension gear is a triumph of patience and expertise by staff at the British Museum. The gear consisted of a series of bars and chains and rings, many of elaborate design. The top ring would have hung from a pole lying across the roof rafter of a hall. The main suspension chain was connected to the ring by a swivel. The lower part of the gear was divided into two, each ending in a hook which went through the cauldron loop handles. The overall length of the gear was about 11 feet 6 inches (3.45m) but it could be shortened. This suspension-gear, like the large cauldron, has many similarities with finds of Roman date. Both may be the product of workshops manned by British craftsmen working in traditional ways. Large bronze cauldrons had been known in Britain for many centuries before the Anglo-Saxon invasions, though the earlier ones differed much in the detail of their structure; as the Irish legends tell, a chief's importance depended in part on the number of cauldrons he owned. For the life of the hall they were a necessity, as in them was seethed the flesh which formed the staple dishes at the daily feast; a great king would need to have many in his possession to feed his numerous retainers.

V

THE GRAVE-GOODS: II

WE MUST NOW consider the gold jewellery and the sword which lay around the keel line immediately to the west of the drinking vessels. There are forty-five gold items, most of which had been mounted on cloth or leather. They include the fittings of a purse-lid and bag, a pair of shoulder-clasps and a number of buckles, strap-mounts and strap-ends in addition to some sword and scabbard fittings. Most of the items are decorated.

Excluding sheet-metal stampings and castings, Anglo-Saxon decoration on small objects of precious metal falls into four main groups. A smooth surface may be chased and the incisions sometimes emphasised, as in the great buckle, with niello-inlay. Niello may be described as a fine black paste which was used to fill the incised lines of a pattern and so to enhance the details by giving them a strong black outline. A surface may also be decorated by the application of filigree-work. Filigree is fine decorative lace-like units built up from delicate metal threads and nodules, the wire threads normally being twisted into slender cables. This type of decoration is rare in the Sutton Hoo jewellery, but as will later be seen is one of the most characteristic features of Kentish work. The other types of decoration differ by the presence of lapidary-work, the enrichment of surfaces by the application of gemstones, coloured glass, shell and perhaps enamel. There are two ways of doing this; the more usual is by the use of cloisonné work, the other by the champlevé technique.

Cloisonné-work involves the attachment by soldering to the plain surface of tiny cell-like cavities which are made by the jeweller from strips of metal bent into suitable shapes; into these cells—or cloisons as they are known—are inserted tiny pieces of the semi-precious stone—usually garnet—which are cut to fit them. The base of each cell is frequently further enhanced by the insertion of gold foil tooled in a diaper-pattern which shows through the translucent stone. An occasional variant is the so-called lidded-cloisonné work; in this some of the cells have a flat plate of gold laid over them instead of the usual garnet-filling and so presenting an alternation of surfaces such as appears in true champlevé. The fourth style is this champlevé, a much rarer technical method. It consists of decoration made by cutting hollows in the surface of the metal into which the jewel or enamel is introduced, so making a true inlay.

One of the most magnificent pieces is the great buckle, some 5 inches (12.5cms) long and weighing nearly 15 oz (415gms). The buckle is thick and looks heavier than this, but it is hollow. The back plate opens on a hinge and can be locked by three catches which connect with three plain domes on the front. The tongue was cast in one with a roundel at its base, which is hinged and moves separately from the tongue. The surface of this great piece is covered with an intricate interlace of conventionalised animal-patterns and the details are further embellished by a generous use of niello-inlay. The loop of the buckle bears two panels of complex ribbon interlace. Forming the shoulders of the buckle-plate are two birds. Certain details of these show that they were made by the same hand as the silver patch on the largest of the hanging bowls.

The jewelled pieces are in quite another artistic style and their finding has greatly widened our ideas of the development and practice of Anglo-Saxon lapidary work. Of prime importance is the great purse-lid. The gold frame, some $7\frac{1}{2}$ inches (19cms) long, is believed to have held a plate of ivory or bone into which the decorative plaques were sunk and fixed with small rivets. The straight top-bar carries three plain gold hinges which were riveted to straps by which it hung from a belt. The frame is jewelled with rectangular cloisons holding small garnet panels sometimes interspersed with insets of blue and white mosaic (millefiori) glass and from the top bar there also project four jewelled tongues. The gracefully-curved lower part of the frame bears in addition a further enrichment of gold filigree-work on its outer edge. A hinged tongue at the base of the frame engaged with a sliding catch on the bag.

The decorative plaques other than the upper central unit fall into pairs, to give a bilateral symmetry. The small roundels have a cloisonné garnet border with a mosaic glass centre, one of which survives. The upper central unit is an intricate animal interlace in which the garnet filling is contrasted with the smooth gold of lidded cloisons. On either side of this is a hexagon with a complex geometric design in garnet and gold. The design includes a border of alternating 'mushroom-cells' and many more of these occur in the inner panels. This mushroom-cell is a cloison with a rounded 'top' and a simple rectangular 'stem' below. This cell-shape also occurs, as will later be seen, in a slightly more elaborate form with double-stepped stem. Centrally below, the paired units each display a hawk seizing a duck and in these the garnet infill is again accompanied by mosaic glass. Outside these a man between two upright biting animals is carried out in garnet and glass cloisonné. Similar scenes are found in Scandinavian helmets of this period. This purse contained a number of gold coins which will be discussed later.

The two clasps also have a special interest, for nothing quite like them is known elsewhere. Each clasp is in two parts which are joined centrally to form a hinged unit by the insertion of a pin; the pin is secured by a tiny chain to one of the half-units. Each half-unit has a central panel with stepped cloisons set diagonally; they contain either garnet or mosaic glass and form a diaper-pattern not before seen in Anglo-Saxon work of the pagan period. As Dr. Bruce-Mitford has pointed out, the nearest English parallels are found in Hiberno-Saxon manuscripts illuminated in Christian Northumbria in Bede's day. These panels are framed in an animal-interlace which also makes use of the lidded-cloison technique. The curved ends of the clasps are in the form of interlocked boars and in the spaces between heads and legs there are filigree fillings. The boars themselves are of garnet with the shoulders in mosaic glass. The gold hinge-pins have animal-head terminals with applied filigree; the eye-sockets, though now blank, were originally picked out in garnet. The curvature of these clasps suggests that they were worn on the shoulder.

To turn now to the smaller pieces, most of which are decorated with garnets. There are two pairs of rectangular mounts. One pair has a two-strand twist arranged as the cable-framework of eight small squares, each containing stepped cloisons. The other pair has a geometric pattern of depressed mushroom cells, that is the form with a double-stepped stem. The T-shaped mount is made in three pieces; the rectangular plate which forms the cross-bar is hinged to the stem, the lower part of which swivels in an arc. The decoration of the cross-bar has simple mushroom cells allied to stepped cells. Two tongue-shaped mounts and a buckle are clearly by the same hand. The design on these pieces is the same and much simpler and bolder than on the other pieces. Much more elaborate are the patterns on a triangular mount, on a buckle with a plain gold loop and on a curved dummy buckle. This latter piece was held by three rivets to a strap; the heads of the rivets are covered by bosses holding garnets. The last two pieces of this group are undecorated, being a strap end and a strap-runner which looks like a buckle without a tongue.

Most of the other gold objects are closely associated with the sword and scabbard. The sword lay in its scabbard and, as was discovered in the laboratory, blade and sheath were so joined together by rust that they could not be separated. The scabbard was made of wood and lined inside with soft skin or fur. The upper part of the scabbard was bound with overlapping bands of fine linen tape. The lower end of the scabbard had textile adhering to it.

Two gold and garnet hemispherical bosses were set on the scabbard about 4 inches (10cms) below the mouth. These bosses have looped shanks like those of metal buttons, and were probably sewn onto a leather strap which ran round the scabbard. On either side of the scabbard and in line with the scabbard bosses were two small master-pieces of the jeweller's art. These are flat-topped pyramids each less than $\frac{3}{4}$ inch (1.9cm) square at the base and less than $\frac{1}{2}$ (1.3cm) high. The angles and upper edges were cut in solid garnets. There are other inlays of mosaic and blue glass.

The sword grip did not survive but the gold fittings did. These are gold cross-bars or guard, two mounts decorated with filigree and the pommel set with garnets. The form of the cloisons on this piece is very different from the rest of the jewellery. The mushroom T-shaped and step-patterned cells which are found on most of the other jewellery suggests that the pommel was made in a different workshop and perhaps at an earlier date.

A number of reconstructions have been made of the body harness which would have carried the sword and purse and incorporated all the pieces of jewellery. Perhaps the most convincing provides for two separate belts. A broader belt fastened with the great gold buckle, with the purse hanging from it on the right-hand side by three short straps. The belt was supported by an adjustable shoulder strap stitched to the back of the belt and passing through the plain gold strap-runner fastened to the front. The tongue-shaped gold and garnet strap-mounts were fixed to the front of this strap, the end of which was fastened by the matching buckle.

The sword was carried by its scabbard bosses on another, narrower,

90

T-shaped strap-distributer mounted on the belt. The other end of the strap passed through the loop of the dummy buckle round the scabbard and was then fixed to the end of the dummy buckle which lay across the lower part of the scabbard. The belt was fastened by the remaining gold and garnet buckle and further embellished by the triangular and four rectangular mounts. The pyramids were probably decorations from the sword knot, that is, two tapes which were fastened to the scabbard and which could be tied around the hilt of the sword.

Gold and garnet jewellery is found much more commonly in Kent than in East Anglia, but there seems little doubt that there was in the early seventh century an East Anglian workshop controlled by an exceptionally skilful master smith. A large number of technical details, including the use of mushroom cells, make it clear that most of this jewellery was produced in a single centre. Some pieces, such as the tongue-shaped mounts and matching buckle, can be identified as the work of a single jeweller. Pieces such as the pyramids could have been produced only by a craftsman of exceptional skill. He probably also made the purse and shoulder clasps. These goldsmiths were assisted by a gem cutter or cutters. Some of the stones set, for instance, in the shoulder clasps would each have taken at least a day to cut and polish. Over four thousand garnets were used in the Sutton Hoo jewellery. The gold itself was probably obtained by melting down old pieces of jewellery or even Byzantine gold coins.

Millefiori or glass mosaic is found in Romano-British contexts and in post Roman objects produced in the Celtic North and West, such as the large hanging bowl. The use of millefiori in pieces such as the shoulder clasps raises the possibility of a Celtic craftsman working in the Sutton Hoo workshop.

Five other small gold items and the contents of the purse have not yet been described. Lying across the sword was a gold strip nearly 4 inches (10cms) long with a ring at the top. The ring and strip were set with garnets *en cabochon*. Soil attached to this gave a very high phosphate reading suggesting that it had been mounted on a rod of bone or ivory. It has been suggested that a detached setting with a garnet and three other small gold mounts belong to this rod. Such a piece is thought to have a ceremonial function.

The purse contained thirty-seven gold coins, three coin blanks and two small gold ingots. All the coins are continental and all are struck at different mints, but none come from the most prolific mints. These

91

mints cover a wide area in what is now France, Belgium, the Rhineland and Switzerland. At the time these coins were being produced, all this land was controlled by the Merovingian Franks. Only one of these coins can be identified with a known king, Theodobert II (A.D. 595–612). A careful study indicates that the majority were produced between 585 and 615. It is likely that the latest coins had been minted by *c.* 620–25. It is possible but unlikely that the two coins might be of *c.* 630. This dating to the late sixth and early seventh centuries was strengthened by analysis which showed that the fineness was over seventy per cent. During the reign of Dagobert (629–39), the fineness declined.

The fact that the latest coins were probably minted *c.* 620–25 gives some help to establish when the hoard, and therefore the whole ship and its contents, was buried. It is thought likely that burial took place *c.* 625–26. The nature of the hoard is a great puzzle. The coins have been carefully selected and it is clearly not a merchant's hoard. It is uncertain how widely, if at all, gold coins were used as currency in England at this time. The coins may have been a diplomatic gift, perhaps from the Merovingian court. It has also been suggested that they were oddments left at the bottom of a treasure chest. Because none come from the prolific, well-known mints, these were rejected when coins were needed to make some payment. Another suggestion is that the thirty-seven coins and three blanks were payment for the forty oarsmen needed to row the ship to the next world. Other theories have also been put forward but none have gained general acceptance.

However these coins came together they are of great importance in helping to date the ship-burial and thus providing a clue to a possible candidate to be commemorated by this great treasure. But before turning to this we must look at the evidence for the structure of the burial chamber and, most controversial of all, the nature of the burial. Was it a cenotaph or did it contain a body?

The burial chamber was probably about 18 feet 3 inches (5.6m) long, of timber, rising perhaps from a plank floor laid across the boat near to the bottom. The simple pitched roof was made of two layers of planks. The lower were laid vertically, resting on the ridge pole and on the gunwales. The outer layer ran horizontally across these. There is no evidence for a door which, if it existed, must have been in an end wall. We do not know the height but it was likely to be 6 feet (nearly 2m) or more to the ridge. This structure stood for about fifty years before the gable ends bulged inwards and the roof fell in causing damage to many of the objects lying below.

The objects had been laid out with great care in the chamber. The walls, or some of them, were hung with linen tapestries decorated with coloured wools. Part at least of the chamber floor was covered with mats. At the west end of the chamber the great stone bar was stood in the centre against the wall, resting on its bronze cup. The iron stand was also leant upright against this wall. It is uncertain if the shield was stood up or laid flat. Near it were the ivory gaming pieces and a bell. On the other side of the stone bar were the wooden bucket and bronze Coptic bowl rested on the floor of the chamber, while the hanging bowl was suspended above from an iron nail. Also hanging in this area was the lyre in its beaver skin bag. The helmet, perhaps wrapped in cloth, was laid on the floor in front of the shield while the stack of ten silver bowls and two silver spoons were placed in front of the bucket. The sword was laid parallel with the keel line and to its side, while the belt and shoulder strap with the purse and great buckle were hung from the roof, perhaps with the sword belt. The two shoulder clasps were apparently placed close together over the keel line on a level with the sword hilt. Beside the sword were laid the spears and angons, one apart from the rest. On the keel line and nearly in the centre of the chamber were placed the drinking vessels covered by a number of carefully folded woollen and leather garments and a piece of wall hanging. Next to them were set the group of silver and bronze vessels, garments, a pillow and small personal objects, all carefully stacked and probably covered with a cloak. The pottery bottle may well have stood with the Anastasius dish. For some reason a second wooden bucket was placed away from the other objects near the edge of the chamber. Then along the eastern wall of the chamber were set the kitchen vessels, the tub, iron-bound wooden bucket and two cauldrons on the floor, while the largest cauldron hung by one handle from a nail hammered into the chamber wall. Perhaps hanging from the roof, looped up to a nail to shorten it, was the cauldron suspension gear.

Did a body lie here, surrounded by this mass of precious, personal and domestic objects? There is space for it—just, between the sceptre and the drinking vessels. It could have been placed there, along the keel line, head to the west or stern of the boat, with sword beside it in the position where so many swords are found in Germanic graves. But despite a very careful search made during the excavations, no trace of a body was found here. Mr. Phillips eventually concluded that this burial was a cenotaph, a memorial to a man, a warrior and probably a king, who was buried elsewhere. His reasons for this were (a) they found no trace of any body, (b) the absence of any personal items such as a finger-ring or pendant or tags from shoe laces or garment laces and (c) the position of the objects, that is, the gold jewellery in the 'body-space'.

It is quite possible that due to the very acid soil conditions and the peculiar conditions within the boat that any body would have totally vanished. The excavators needed to remove the gold jewellery rapidly and however carefully they looked as they excavated each piece, the methods they had to use were against the recovery of minute scraps of bone or the recognition of subtle changes in the soil. Other rich burials have been found apparently without personal items such as rings or garment tags. The position of the gold jewellery is more difficult. If a skeleton is drawn into the 'body space' along the keel line, the gold fittings of the belts and shoulder strap, including the gold buckle and purse lie about the knees, an unlikely position in which to be buried. But this can be explained away by suggesting they were hung from the roof, a theory which accounts for other curious features of the layout. But the position of the shoulder-clasps is a difficult one to explain. They lay side-by-side, about $1\frac{1}{2}$ inches (3.8cms) apart. If a body had filled this space, they would have lain on the body between the thighs.

After the war, in an attempt to settle the problem, a number of objects were analysed to see if they had a high phosphate content as could be expected if a body had filled this space. When the boat was re-excavated in 1965-67 tests were made inside it. Areas of high phosphate were found, some of which could be explained by the presence of other bone or ivory objects such as the gaming pieces with the shield. But there was sufficient evidence to convince Dr. Bruce-Mitford and some other archaeologists that a body had been laid in the 'body-space' at the time the ship was buried, perhaps on a carpet or perhaps raised on a bed or low staging. Beds have been found in graves on the Continent and in East Anglian graves in the seventh century as at Study Camp 5 in Cambridgeshire.

Professor Evison agrees with the presence of a body which she would place further east than the position proposed by Dr. Bruce-Mitford, so that the drinking horns and associated pad of garments were placed over the legs. She suggests that the body lay on its side,

94

with the sword hilt near the shoulder. The shoulder clasps would then be at the shoulder, and the belt, with gold buckle and purse around the waist. The purse was upside-down because of the position of the body. She has further suggested that the body and some other objects were enclosed within a large wooden coffin 10 feet 9 inches (3.27m) long and 5 feet 6 inches (1.67m) wide. Her main evidence for this is two rows of iron cleats either side of the body. Dr. Bruce-Mitford interpreted them as fittings connected with the burial chamber. Such a large coffin would contain the body with the helmet and the silver bowls and spoons on either side of the head. The sword too, lay within the coffin and beside it the special spear with its shaft broken in half; the other end of the shaft and the ferrule was placed on the other side of the body. The drinking vessels and the stack of vessels and garments found covered by the Anastasius dish were also within this great wooden chest. The Anastasius dish and the pottery bottle were, she suggests, set on top of the coffin at its eastern end. When the coffin lid collapsed, smashed perhaps when the burial chamber roof fell in, the Anastasius dish dropped down onto the pile of objects below while the bottle landed on its side nearby. This would leave outside the coffin the lines of objects against the gable walls and the iron-bound bucket just to the south of the coffin.

But not all will accept an inhumation burial within the boat. One area of high phosphate content recorded was on the Anastasius dish. The excavators had noted here what they thought was a piece of bone. The phosphate content is higher than could have been reached by a single piece of bone. Some have suggested that this represents the remains of an over-cooked piece of meat placed in the burial. Dr Vierck and others feel that here were the cremated remains of the dead man placed in a silver dish as befits a man of rank. Barrow Nos. 3 and 4 at Sutton Hoo had contained cremation burials accompanied by unburnt grave-goods and similar instances have been found elsewhere. Unfortunately we can never now be sure, but the evidence for the presence of a body, be it an inhumation or a cremation, is strong, and the cenotaph theory is now the least likely answer, though a number of people still believe it.

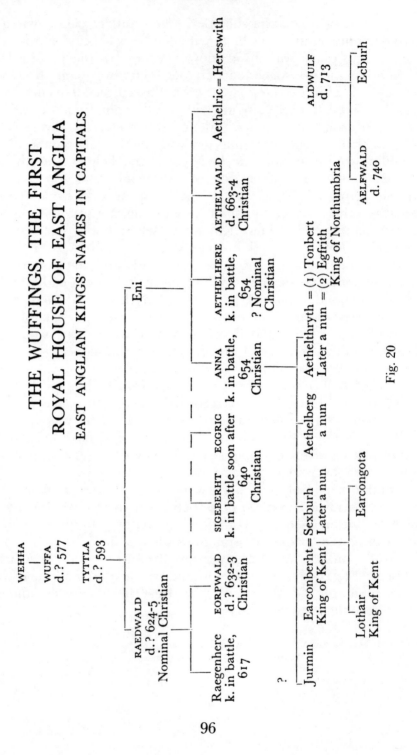

THE WUFFINGS, THE FIRST
ROYAL HOUSE OF EAST ANGLIA
EAST ANGLIAN KINGS' NAMES IN CAPITALS

WEHHA
|
WUFFA
d.? 577
|
TYTTLA
d.? 593
|
RAEDWALD
d.? 624-5
Nominal Christian

Eni

Raegenhere   EORPWALD   SIGEBERHT   ECGRIC   ANNA   AETHELHERE   AETHELWALD   Aethelric = Hereswith
k. in battle,   d.? 632-3   k. in battle soon after   k. in battle,   k. in battle,   k. in battle,   d. 663-4
617   Christian   640   654   654   654   Christian
                                 Christian   Christian   ? Nominal
                                                                                     Christian

?

Jurmin   Earconberht = Sexburh   Aethelberg   Aethelthryth = (1) Tonbert   ALDWULF
         King of Kent Later a nun   a nun   Later a nun = (2) Egfrith   d. 713
                                               King of Northumbria
                                                                                       AELFWALD
                                                                                       d. 740

Lothair   Earcongota   Ecburh
King of Kent

Fig. 20

96

VI

THE BURIAL:

WHO WAS HE?

THE FIRST essential to be determined is the status of the burial. Is it royal? No certainly identifiable burials of this period have been discovered in Britain so there is no yard-stick for comparison here. The burial is so much richer than any so far discovered in western Europe that a royal status is assumed by the majority of archaeologists. Not only are the number and quality of the gold pieces unparalleled, but no other burial has produced anything like the sixteen pieces of imported East Mediterranean silver. Indeed few comparable pieces of silver have been found in continental princely graves. Bede, writing about a century later than the date of the ship burial, records the use of silver dishes at the court of Oswald of Northumbria (633-41). We are therefore dealing with an exceptional assemblage and one which most archaeologists would accept as royal. But even if it is royal, is it necessarily the burial of a king and, if so, which king?

Unfortunately we do not know how to identify a king. We assume he would have been very wealthy and that he would have had certain items of regalia which would proclaim his position to the world. The gold jewellery decorating the sword belt and the broader belt and shoulder strap would have conferred dignity on a figure and is probably a mark of rank. So too, almost certainly, are the shoulder-clasps. Although unmatched in any Germanic context, such pieces provide a link with the Roman Empire for shoulder-clasps were worn as a part of Imperial costume as well as cavalry dress. This interest in Roman badges of authority was expressed by Germanic royalty in a number of ways. Bede noted it when writing of Edwin of Northumbria (616/7-32) how 'whenever he passed through the streets on foot the standard known to the Romans as a *Tufa*, and to the English as a *Tuf*, was also carried in front of him.' We do not know what the *Tuf*

97

looked like, nor the other two types of standard which announced Edwin's dignity.

A possible use for the iron stand is as such a standard. As it was buried at the west end of the chamber, it probably had some sort of ceremonial function. It could be carried and it could have been stuck upright in the ground. Perhaps it was decorated with feathers or branches stuck in the iron grill, perhaps as some have suggested, it was a lamp; such a use would not preclude a ceremonial role.

The third, and to many the most important, piece likely to have been a badge of authority is the great stone bar, surmounted at one end with a bronze stag and at the other with a bronze cup. It has been interpreted as a sceptre. Because of its great weight it is thought the king would have sat with the cup resting over a knee.

Consular sceptres or rods of authority are known from the Roman Empire in the fifth and sixth century. The evidence for the use of sceptres by Germanic kings at this time is very slight but we know that sceptres were becoming more important as badges of kingship in Carolingian times. Even if it were not a sceptre, it is difficult to conceive of any useful purpose for the great stone bar. Dr. Bruce-Mitford has suggested that the whetstone in Germanic myth was the equivalent of a thunderbolt wielded by the supreme sky-god in his capacity as ruler of all and guardian of justice.

If one accepts that these pieces are regalia belonging to a king, is it possible to put a name to that king? It is unlikely that any but a king of East Anglia would have been buried at Sutton Hoo.

The East Anglian royal house was known as Wuffingas, that is, the descendants of Uffa or Wuffa. It is difficult to date these early East Anglian kings and to be sure of their relationships with certainty. The first East Anglian king of this dynasty, perhaps dating to the mid sixth century, was Wehha, father of Wuffa. According to a Genealogy written down in the ninth century, Tyttla succeeded Wuffa. He had two sons, Raedwald, who probably became king in *c*.599, and Eni. Raedwald had two sons, Raegenhere, who died in battle 616/7 and Eorpwald, who succeeded to the throne in about 624 and who was killed in 627/8. Sigeberht, who was Raedwald's wife's child by an earlier marriage and apparently disliked by his stepfather, became king three years after Eorpwald's murder. The kingdom seems to have been divided between him and Ecgric, who has been identified as possibly Aethelric, a son of Eni. If so, Ecgric and Sigeberht would have been cousins. Both were killed fighting Penda of Mercia in

636/7. The East Anglian throne was then held by three other sons of Eni, Anna (636/7–654), Aethelhere (654–655) and Aethelwald (655–663/4).

For many years scholars argued the claims of these last three kings to be the one associated with the great ship burial as the coins in the purse were then thought to date to *c*. 650. The recent re-dating suggests that we must consider the period 615–635. There are therefore four possible kings: Raedwald, Eorpwald, Sigeberht and Ecgric. At least one scholar has suggested however a preference for Ragenhere as she believes it to be a royal, but not a king's burial.

Raedwald came to the throne in *c*.599 and within fifteen years had become a powerful leader. Before 618 he became converted to Christianity while visiting Kent. Aethelberht of Kent had close links with the Merovingian lands and may well have given Raedwald the two spoons as a christening present. Aethelberht was *bretwalda* or high-king, the third English king to hold this title. The precise significance of this is unknown, but the man who bore the title was in some way the most prominent of the English rulers at the time. Aethelberht died in 618 but Raedwald may already have replaced him as *bretwalda*. Certainly in 616/7 he was powerful enough to fight and slay Aethelfrith of Northumbria and secure the throne for Edwin of Deira who had lived at Raedwald's court for a number of years.

Raegenhere, Raedwald's son, was killed in this battle. Raedwald's Christian convictions were not very strong. When he returned to East Anglia he came again under the influence of his pagan wife and members of his court. To ensure the best of both worlds, he erected two altars in a temple, one for Christian worship and the other for pagan. After his death in *c*.624 his son Eorpwald succeeded to the throne of East Anglia but the position of *bretwalda* passed to Edwin of Northumbria. Both Edwin and Eorpwald were converted to Christianity in 627. Eorpwald was soon murdered by the pagan Ricberht who may have become king for the next three years until he was deposed in 630 by Sigeberht. Sigeberht had been converted to Christianity many years before becoming king. He soon abdicated and retired to a monastery he had founded. When war with Penda of Mercia threatened he was dragged from his monastery to help lead the East Anglian levies with his cousin Ecgric; both died in battle in 636/7. It is not known if Ecgric was Christian or pagan.

Sigeberht and Ecgric were succeeded by the Christian king Anna. It is unlikely that the good Christian Sigeberht, if his body was recovered

Fig. 21.   How the gold regalia may have been worn

from the battlefield, was given a great pagan burial. It is more likely that he returned to his monastery. It is perhaps unlikely that Anna would have buried Ecgric in this way but not impossible. Eorpwald too must be a possibility, though his murder after conversion suggests he may not have been held in high esteem. Many feel that Raedwald is the most likely candidate for this great burial. His ambivalent attitude to Christianity could explain the presence of Christian objects, the bowls and spoons, in an essentially pagan burial. If the great stone bar or sceptre is accepted as Raedwald's symbol of authority as *bretwalda* created for him in his royal workshop, it must greatly strengthen the case for the burial being that of Raedwald. If this sceptre were part of the regalia of the East Anglian royal house, it might be expected to pass to the next king. But the position of *bretwalda* could not be inherited, it passed to the most powerful king of the time and there is no suggestion that any badge of rank passed from one *bretwalda* to another. Although the claims of both Ecgric and Eorpwald cannot be dismissed, Raedwald, the most powerful of East Anglian kings, must surely be the most likely to be buried in the most prominent of the barrows in the cemetery.

VII

NORTH SEA CROSSINGS

FOR UPWARDS of 250 years, North German pirates and settlers were crossing the North Sea from the Continent to Britain. By what route did they come? To this question, no satisfactory answer has been given in the past. It has, indeed, been generally assumed that Angles crossed from Schleswig to the Humber and the Wash, Saxons, Frisians and Jutes to the Thames Estuary and the Channel shore, as well as to the Wash. The problem, in fact, has hardly been seen as a problem. They were seamen, they had sea-going vessels and so they crossed. But such an assumption avoids real difficulties, for to understand the various phases of the Anglo-Saxon settlement, and particularly the East Anglian settlement-pattern, it is necessary to have a clear picture of how the settlers got there. Their Continental homes have already been discussed, and we are here concerned only with the seafaring problems which confronted them. We have reviewed at some length the ships used in these North Sea crossings and found that the normal vessel was a rowing galley of some 60-80 feet (18-24m) long, somewhat cranky and ill-suited to survive a North Sea gale. We must now try to estimate the composition of the boats' companies and, for this purpose, the Nydam ship with its thirty oars, will be used as the standard type.

It is easy to see that, in the earlier days of piracy, such a boat could have carried a crew of from sixty to eighty men, so that reliefs were available for the oars. But when, in the true Migration Period, family parties began to cross, as is certain from Bede's account. as well as from the graves and their contents, the problem changed. The captain of the galley would generally be the leading man of a village- or family-group. The thirty oarsmen would be his kinsmen and dependents, some adolescent and some older men. With them would be perhaps as many girls and women, together with a number of small children. The ship would certainly be very full and if, in addition to food and water, some bulky personal possessions were also brought, it would probably be uncomfortably so. The later Viking vessels of approximately the same length normally carried from three to five times as many men as there were oars, but these later vessels were proportionately much broader and had higher freeboard—i.e. higher sides above the waterline—so that eighty persons would be a very full company for the Nydam ship. And with a mixed party, though many of the women could take an oar for a time in an emergency, the general practice would doubtless be not to overwork the oarsmen.

Severely limiting, too, was the absence of clock, chart or compass. All navigation, in a sea notorious for its mists, strong winds, shoals and swift tides, would have to be by dead reckoning. And what could an Anglian farmer-fisher from the Baltic coast of Schleswig know of the topography of the former Roman province of Britain? Certainly after a century or more of piracy or trading, most North German seamen of the North Sea coasts would have some knowledge, either by experience or by hearsay, of Britain's general position and configuration. But this would have been learned while stalking and raiding, or by serving aboard Roman merchantmen trading between the Rhine or the north Gaulish ports such as Boulogne, and the south-east coasts of Britain. It would seem, therefore, that to make a desired landfall, they would first wish to reach those Continental coasts from which they knew a safe passage to Britain could be made with some certainty.

The leaders, then, of parties from Schleswig, both because of the heavily-laden ships and of the limits of their topographical knowledge, would incline to make first, or be forced to make first, a coasting voyage to the Low Countries. From there they could cross the Narrow Seas by a comparatively short passage. And, indeed, on a clear summer's day, the English cliffs are to be seen from Cap Gris Nez, so that even the most cautious shipman could be assured of a fair landfall. We may also go further and say that, except by accident of weather or ignorance, no direct passage from North Schleswig to England was ever made at this time. It was, normally speaking, an impossible voyage to make without a steady north-east wind and a lifting square-sail, which they had not got, and could only have succeeded by good fortune and under exceptionally favourable conditions. Of this the truth may easily be demonstrated.

To grasp the difficulty of the North Sea crossing, either direct or by the coastwise route, it is necessary to choose a specific date in the year and, working with the sun and tide data for that and following days, make a theoretical crossing. Here it is enough to summarise such a coastwise voyage, as well as the almost impossible direct crossing. But in an appendix, the details of the coasting voyage to England, from Esbjerg on the south-west coast of Jutland, are given and some attempt is made to show how specific difficulties would be overcome. For this purpose, it has been assumed that the crew would row a vessel of Nydam type at a steady speed of 5 knots for periods up to six hours or more. But this is fairly certainly an overestimate for these migrating family-parties, and as is explained in more detail in the appendix, the true rate should be about 3 knots, and that only for a comparatively limited period.

The direct passage may first be considered. As conveniently high tides occur on or about April 24 at Esbjerg, this date for the departure has been chosen for, if the season is good, the fair weather is likely to persist for several days. Leaving Esbjerg at dawn (high water 03.30 hours and sunrise about 04.10 hours)[1] and rowing at 5 knots on a course of about west-south-west for Spurn Head at the mouth of the Humber, the tides will modify the estimated position by several miles from time to time. But if there is no wind and the steered course never varies, the end of the journey will be some 13 miles south-south-east of the objective and the ship will come ashore between Saltfleet and Mablethorpe on the Lincolnshire coast at about 20.30 hours on April 26 (sunset at 19.14) as darkness falls. This means that thirty men will row at a steady 5 knots for sixty-five hours, while the leader steers a perfect compass course without a compass and all the time there is no wind.

To attempt a somewhat more realistic estimate than this impossibly swift and accurate crossing, another journey between these points was plotted. But this time the rowing speed was reduced to 3 knots and it was further assumed that the vessel lay to a sea-anchor from sunset to sunrise. In the absence of wind, therefore, it was tide-drifted only during the night. With these altered conditions, a ship which left Esbjerg at dawn on April 24 would reach Sutton-on-Sea in Lincolnshire about midday on May 2, a passage of 8½ days. And again this

---

[1] All local times are reduced to Greenwich Mean Time (G.M.T.), and the twenty-four-hour clock is used. All distances by sea are given in nautical miles, i.e. minutes of latitude, or about 1⅐ English Statute Miles (E.S.M.).

presupposes that a true course was steered whenever the crew was rowing and that no wind blew. These conditions are clearly impossible; and even an open-sea passage of $8\frac{1}{2}$ days would not be undertaken with a heavily-laden ship, when a comparatively easy coasting voyage was possible. Had such crossings been attempted, they would almost inevitably have ended in disaster.

The coasting voyage down the West Schleswig coast and westward along the East and West Frisian island-fringe to Texel, lasted from April 24 to midday on May 3. This passage was again based on a rowing speed of 5 knots and a daily passage; no allowances were made for bad weather, mishap, sickness or ignorance of local waters. From Texel, two courses were open. One was to put to sea on a course due west and make the Wash. Holding this course, again at 5 knots, the ship landed on Sheringham beach in twenty-four hours, a landfall a few miles south of the estimated position, The other alternative was to continue coastwise southward from Texel to Flushing or Dunkirk, and cross the Narrow Seas more rapidly. From Flushing, it was calculated a passage to Harwich, with the same ideal conditions, would have taken $16\frac{1}{2}$ hours, so that by this route, a ship which left Esbjerg on April 24 at 08.00 hours reached Harwich on May 7 at 20.30 hours, some fourteen days. By extending the coastal voyage for another day down the Belgian coast, the open-sea crossing would be considerably reduced; made from the neighbourhood of Calais on a day of good visibility, land would never be out of sight.

It is certain, therefore, that with an average rowing speed of 3 knots, together with all the delays due to weather, to human frailty and to the condition of the ship, most passages from Schleswig to East Anglia must have taken some two months. In bad seasons, it may well have been six months. And many more must have failed altogether. Some of these parties may have been lost by shipwreck and drowning. Others, by forced choice due to sickness, lack of fortitude or by the loss of their ship, may have settled on any part of the continental coast as far west as Calais, if only the local inhabitants were not too hostile. Evidence for scattered settlements of this kind has been found, for cremation urns of early fifth-century type, deriving from the homeland to the north, are well known both in Belgium and South Holland. It is clear, also that such lengthy voyages would lead to some intercourse between the travellers and the local people, for food from time to time would have to be obtained. Odd trinkets might well be acquired at the same time and the occurrence of an odd Saxon or

Rhenish brooch in a purely Anglian village-cemetery in England may mean no more than such a trivial commercial contact.

So far we have dealt only with the parties who put to sea from the West Schleswig coast. But the centres of Anglian population seem rather to have lain in the eastern half of Schleswig and many, if not most, Anglian ships were doubtless kept in the fjords and bays of the tideless Baltic coast, to which they were better suited. It is less easy to decide how these ships made their journeys. Probably enough, many of the parties may have embarked at some staithe in the Schlei Fjord or the Als Sound and made the journey round the Jutish coast. Other parties perhaps crossed to the west coast by land, an average journey of some 40 miles and there met their ships which had been taken round Jutland by a skeleton crew. This preliminary voyage would have been along the shore of the Little Belt and the Cattegat, through the Liim Fjord—in those days open, though later in part silted up— and south along the west coast of Jutland to the North Frisian island-fringe. By this route the comparatively hazardous passage round the Skaw would be avoided and, indeed, some distance saved, a matter of some importance when rowing was the motive power. Nevertheless, this preliminary passage would add nearly another month to the overall time of the voyage to England.

Saxons from the Elbe estuary and the East Frisian shore would have followed the same coastwise route, but for them the journey would be somewhat shorter. And, indeed, their landings in south and south-east England point strongly to their having coasted as far as Cap Gris Nez, though some may have crossed to the Wash and so penetrated to the Midlands by the major rivers, as Leeds' studies have shown. During these voyages, there must, under these conditions, have been much contact between Angles and Saxons on passage. Under the hazards of travel, slight differences of pronunciation of a more or less common tongue, the wearing of different brooches, and other minor cultural variations, must all have been forgotten; mutual aid and fraternisation would lead to different groups joining forces to establish a footing on the English shore. This point needs no labouring and the occurrence, particularly of Saxon-type urns and brooches in the predominantly Anglian eastern counties, need cause no surprise. More odd, indeed, would have been their entire absence. Traces of Anglian culture found from time to time in predominantly Saxon territory may be similarly explained.

One other uncertain factor must be mentioned. These hypothetical

107

voyages have been assessed in relation to the present-day coastline. Now it is certain that, during the Migration Period and, apparently, for some centuries before it began, conditions on the Frisian shore had been deterioriating due to the encroachment of the sea. Archaeological investigations have shown that, in the areas close to the coast, homesteads were wont to be built on artificial mounds—*terpen* as they are called—which lifted the houses above the water-table of the surrounding marshland. Indeed, it is well-recognised that this slow submergence of the land of an expanding people set up population-pressures which were one of the causes of such large-scale migration. Tentative reconstructions have been made of the coastline as it then was. It is fairly clear that many of the East and West Frisian islands were larger than they are today and the mainland behind the island-fringe was less indented by great estuaries. Conversely, the Belgian coast, or at least the dry mainland, lay rather inshore of its present-day line. But though the topographical detail of today differs in many ways from that of 1,500 years ago, it is unlikely that there is any essential difference in the basic conditions. The shore would still be low-lying with impeding banks and tidal channels between the islands and mainland. Sunrise and sunset, times of high and low water and the tidal streams would not be significantly different.

The passages therefore have been worked out for a route outside the islands, so that a local variation in inshore channels does not invalidate the calculations. It is probable enough that, when going ashore for the night, the leader would take advantage of the shelter of a channel-entrance. Saxon leaders who knew the coast well would doubtless use inshore channels for daytime passages, when a stiff onshore breeze was blowing. But it is unlikely that an Angle from East Schleswig would know them with sufficient intimacy, particularly as his seafaring in the tideless Baltic was but poor preparation for the tide-rips and rushing streams of the Frisian coast.

APPENDIX

To make clear the duration of a voyage from Schleswig to England, a detailed itinerary is given below. This has been calculated, as I have said above, on the assumption that the crew could row a vessel of Nydam type at a steady speed of 5 knots for periods up to six hours or more. But as this seemed certainly to be an over-estimate, I have discussed the matter at some length with the coxswain and some senior members of the Caister lifeboat crew, as well as with a former coxswain who, in his younger days had worked in the beach yawls as well as in pulling lifeboats. The agreed opinion was that an average speed of 3 knots was the best that could be achieved, unless there were frequent reliefs. The further opinion was that, unless the voyage were urgent, the whole company would tend to rest for a day after a fairly long pull, more especially if the weather was not very good. This means that the following itinerary is impossibly fast and should, for normal crossings, be at least trebled. Many crossings would have taken much longer and a bad season would have meant considerable delay in reaching the final destination.

I have chosen Esbjerg on the south-west coast of Jutland as the most northerly point from which Anglian departures were made. Many, however, must have left the mainland coast at points behind the fringe of North Frisian islands, thus reducing the crossing-time by some days. The times of high water at the named places are taken from the tables of tidal instances given in various nautical almanacs, my own being *Reed's Nautical Almanac* (Sunderland, published annually). The direction and speed of tidal currents have been calculated from the series of charts in *Brown's Tidal Streams for the Whole of the British Coasts, Ireland and North Sea* (Thirteenth Edition, Glasgow, 1952). An adequate explanation of the modern theory of tide-formation, and the co-tidal lines centring on the various amphidromic points in the North Sea, may be found in Doodson and Warburg's *Admiralty Manual of Tides* (London 1941). Admiralty Chart No. 301, *British Islands and Adjacent Waters*, showing co-tidal and co-range lines, may also be consulted. This chart makes quite clear that, during a passage from the Schleswig-Holstein coasts to northern East Anglia or the Humber, two such systems are traversed, the coastal points of their meeting lying between Texel and Terschelling on the north coast of Holland and near Cromer in Norfolk. Therefore, during a crossing from Schleswig to the Wash, following the coastwise route, the voyage would begin in system No. 2—numbered southward from the Norwegian coast—pass into No. 3 off the Dutch coast and return to No. 2 on the north Norfolk coast. Because of this, the crew would experience great changes in the range of tidal rise and fall, perplexing to a Baltic seaman. There are also considerable differences in the rates of tidal streams. Thus, on the east coast of Norfolk, during spring tides, the southbound flood-stream may run as fast as 4 knots for some hours. Against this a Nydam-type ship could make no headway. How far these difficulties and the determination of individual parties to press on, or stay near the first landfall, influenced the choice of settlement-site will never be known. But it is clear that in some such way, much of the cultural admixture which is apparent in the distribution of urn-types and trinkets, may be explained. Together with the suggestions already made above, this gives three distinct ways in which admixture took place.

It is only when one works out the details of crossings by various routes that the real difficulties become apparent. Using the relevant data from almanac and tide-chart, I have chosen to begin on a date late in April, when the spring tides are high and the weather is often suited to such a voyage. The 'unit of travel' is a single daily passage at a rowing speed of 5 knots with no allowance made for bad weather, sickness, damage to ship or error due to lack of knowledge of the coast. But the absence of clock, compass and chart must again be stressed. A further complication has also to be noted. Standard time in Denmark and Germany—based of course on the sun's passage—is one hour ahead of Greenwich and, in Holland 20 minutes. On the West Schleswig coast, sunrise and sunset are roughly 36 minutes earlier than at Greenwich. All times shown below, therefore, are reduced to G.M.T. Allowances have also been made for the different speeds of tidal streams at springs and neaps. Distances are given in nautical miles with English Statute Miles (E.S.M.) sometimes shown in brackets. The narrative is cast in the form of a log and, for convenience in presentation, two ships are supposed to have sailed in company.

April 24. Left Esbjerg at about 08.00 hours as the tide turned to flood south along the Schleswig coast. It reached a speed of 2 knots and then slackened, turning again to ebb NNW at about 14.00 hours. The east coast of Sylt was reached, a distance of 38 miles (44 E.S.M.).

April 25. Left Sylt at about 08.00 near low water. 6 hours' rowing brought the ship to the north coast of Pellworm.

April 26. Left Pellworm at about 09.00 near low water. 6 hours' rowing on the flood tide made Büsum on the NE side of the Elbe estuary entrance.

110

In the approaches to the Elbe, conditions changed. The bay of the estuary had to be crossed. A theoretical passage, similar to those already made, would be to Wangeroog, the most easterly of the East Frisian islands. From Büsum, this would be reached by setting a direct course to the Scharhorn and then across the Weser-Jade entrance to Wangeroog. To do this Büsum would have to be left 1–2 hours before high water. The last of the flood would at first make progress slow, but would soon ease and then a favourable ebb would enable the ship to reach Wangeroog about high water or a little later. But on April 27, sunrise at Büsum was not until about 04.00 hours and sunset at about 18.50. Therefore, as the morning high water was at 03.19 hours, it would have meant putting to sea two hours or more before sunrise. On the afternoon tide, leaving Büsum at about 14.00 hours would have meant that the Scharhorn would not have been reached until near sunset, with another 20 miles across the Weser-Jade entrance to traverse mainly in darkness, which was impossible. Therefore—

April 27. Left Büsum at about 07.00 hours at half ebb and, passing down the channel towards the Scharhorn, entered the main Elbe channel at low water, whence the flood-tide took the ship to Cuxhaven by high water at 13.00 hours.

April 28. Left Cuxhaven at high water at about 04.00, which was also the time of sunrise. Off Scharhorn at about 06.15 and changed course for Wangeroog, where arrived about low water, a little before 10.00.

April 29. Left Wangeroog (east end) soon after dawn at high water (sunrise, 04.04) and steered W outside the island, to reach the W end of Norderney at about low water, 11.30 hours, passing inside the island in slack water and on the first of the flood.

April 30. Left Norderney at about 05.00 (high water) and steered N outside Juist on the ebb. There was scarcely time to make Schiermonnikoog before the tide turned, so went ashore at Rottum.

Between Rottum and Texel the tides are difficult, due to the contact of two rotary tidal-wave systems. Furthermore, at low water *inside* the West Frisian islands, the ebb-stream outside still runs W for a time, and correspondingly, east after high water. Accordingly—

May 1. Left Rottum at about 06.00 hours when the tide-stream slackened. Steered W to Schiermonnikoog and then to Ameland. Owing to the earlier times of high water towards the W went ashore on Ameland at about low water (10.00 hours).

May 2. Left Ameland at about 06.30 hours (sunrise 04.20) when the tide was slack and, though progress at first was slow, it soon improved with an increasing westbound stream along the Vlieland coast and so across to the west side of Texel. The tide just enabled the ship to reach the S end of the island before it began to run W at about 13.00 hours.

Two possible courses were now open. The first was to push out to sea and cross directly to the north Norfolk coast and the Wash. The other was to coast still further south to Flushing, or even to Dunkirk, and then cross the Narrow Seas to Harwich. Of these, Ship No. 1 took the open-sea route and Ship No. 2 coasted.

SHIP No. 1
May 4. Left Texel at about 10.30 hours steering due W, when the tide was running roughly W. Rowing for 12 hours at 5 knots, the estimated position was about 53° N 30 ° E. But the tide, moving in turn W, NW, N, NE, E, SE and S for various periods and at different speeds, had carried the ship roughly in a semicircle in relation to its estimated course, leaving it on that course but some 3 miles to the E of its supposed position, which was about half way across. Continuing to row for another 12 hours at 5 knots, the estimated position was a few miles N of Cromer. This time the tide was rather more helpful. The ship was carried in turn NW, N and S, leaving it $3\frac{1}{2}$ miles SW of its estimated position, i.e., on Sheringham beach.

From Esbjerg to Sheringham, therefore, by this route, had taken 12 days, including an open-sea crossing of 24 hours rowing steadily at 5 knots and steering an accurate course, in practice an impossible feat.

SHIP No. 2
May 4. Left Texel at about 05.00, when the northbound stream slackened a little after high water. Steering S with a southbound stream, reached Ymuiden in slack water at about 10.00 hours.

May 5. Left Ymuiden at slack water at about 05.00 and with some hours of favourable tide, reached the Hook of Holland at about 11.00 hours.

May 6. Left the Hook in slack water at about 06.00 and steered outside the islands with a favourable tide towards Walcheren, reaching its SW point at about 12.00, just after the tide had turned. The east-bound flood then carried the ship into Flushing Bay.

May 7. Left Flushing at sunrise (04.00) and steered towards Harwich (roughly W by N ½N). At first the tide set W and NW but later turned to SW. At the end of 6 hours rowing, the ship had advanced 30 miles direct and had been set some 7 miles to the SW of its estimated position. During most of the next 6 hours' rowing, the tide was setting NE, so that the ship's actual position was roughly some 5 miles NE of estimate. For the next two hours, the tide was nearly slack, first setting NE and then SW, so that the divergences from true course cancelled each other. Finally, in two to three hours, on the SW-running flood-tide, the ship reached Harwich at about 20.30. Sunset that day was at about 19.30, so that dusk was rapidly falling as the shore was approached.

Ship No. 2, therefore, had spent 14 days voyaging from Esbjerg to Harwich including an open-sea crossing of over 16 hours.

These imaginary passages, worked out with chart and almanac, at an impossibly fast rowing speed and with the assumption of a knowledge of destination, good landing-places and tide-conditions, have shown the theoretically possible minimum time in which the passages could be made. It will be noted that the rowing speed has only just enabled certain more arduous crossings, such as the Elbe estuary, the Weser-Jade estuary and the Narrow Seas, to be made in fairly good time. At the more realistic speed of 3 knots, with all allowances made for bad weather, mishap, sickness, ignorance of local waters and the needs of travel, the minimum allowance of two months or more is fully justified. And, apart from those families which stayed on the continental shore, there must have been many deaths during the various voyages. Doubtless the dead were buried with due ceremony where possible, and so the exotic cremation urns would stay to mark the temporary halt of a migrant group.

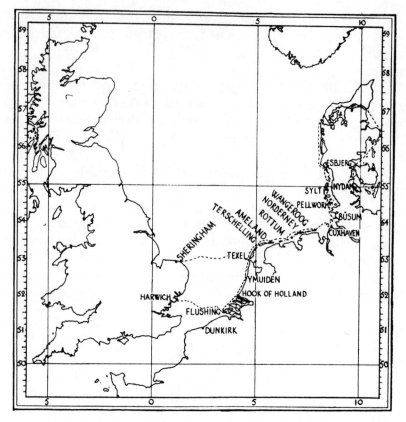

Fig. 22.   Chart of the North Sea, showing coastwise routes

VIII

THE ANGLO-SAXON SETTLEMENT

OF EAST ANGLIA

IN THE LAST twenty-five years there has been a great upsurge of interest in Anglo-Saxon studies and, in particular, in the early part of the period. The discovery and excavation of new sites, the re-examination of old finds and the rare written record have led many scholars to challenge old ideas.

The documentary evidence for early Anglo-Saxon England is scanty and difficult to interpret, while many of the dates given for events in the fifth and sixth centuries are inaccurate. The *Anglo-Saxon Chronicle* is a late ninth century work, although it incorporates earlier annals perhaps first written down in the seventh century. Bede's *History of the English Church and People* was completed in 731. Among the earlier sources he used was *The Ruin of Britain* by Gildas, written in South Wales about 540. These and other documents provide a general framework for the start and consolidation of the Anglo-Saxon settlement of Britain, but events in East Anglia are virtually ignored until Bede takes up the story of Raedwald in the early seventh century, and therefore are of little help in trying to establish how and when the Anglo-Saxon kingdom of East Anglia came into being.

Archaeological evidence is the main source for any discussion of the settlement and development of the kingdom of East Anglia. But the evidence is heavily biased in favour of stray finds of metal-work and of cemeteries, the latter usually only partly excavated and imperfectly recorded. Much systematic, detailed archaeological fieldwork and excavation is needed to determine how valid is the picture summarised in the next few pages.

In the late fourth century Roman Britain, in common with the rest of the Western Empire, was under pressure. Scots from Ireland and Picts from Scotland were attacking western and northern Britain while the East and South-east coasts were raided by Saxon pirates, probably

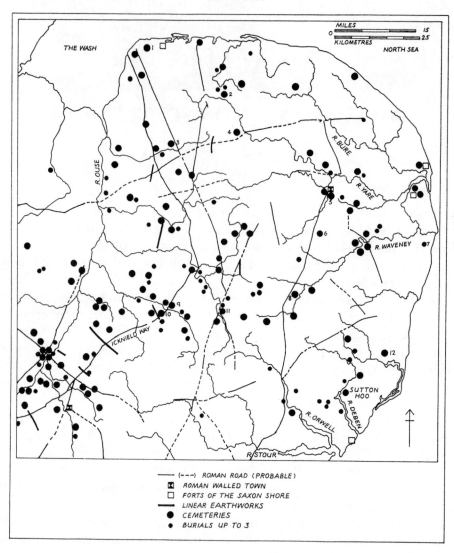

Fig. 23.   East Anglian cemeteries
            Key to numbered cemeteries
            1 Thornham   7 Pakefield
            2 Pensthorpe   8 Eye
            3 Castle Acre   9 West Stow
            4 Spong Hill   10 Lackford
            5 Caistor by Norwich   11 Ixworth
            6 Morning Thorpe   12 Snape

116

from northern Germany. A series of forts from the Wash to the Solent protected naval bases for ships of the British fleet which attempted to prevent the Saxon pirates landing in Britain. These forts held mobile garrisons which could be quickly deployed to attack those raiders which successfully avoided the Roman naval vessels. By the end of the fourth century this line of forts was under the control of a single army commander, the Count of the Saxon Shore.

For the Romano-British people living in these coastal areas life must have been difficult living with the possibility of sudden pirate raids on their homesteads. In addition to these hazards there is evidence for an economic decline in the fourth century which led, around the year 400, to a collapse of the pottery industry. Many other industries, less well represented in the archaeological record, must have suffered too. There was also a breakdown in the monetary economy. Few coins minted after A.D. 400 have been found in Britain and earlier fourth century coins probably remained in circulation for some years after 400. The use of coinage in Britain ceased within the first two or three decades of the fifth century.

The withdrawal of Roman troops and administrators in the early years of the fifth century left the people of Britain in control of their own destiny.

It is very difficult to identify and date the settlements of the native population in the fifth century, particularly in eastern Britain. Pottery vessels and metal objects produced in the late fourth century must have remained in use into the fifth century. But as these were broken, they must have been replaced by the products of local craftsmen. Many vessels were probably made in wood or leather and have failed to survive. Others, in the absence of coinage, are difficult to date. Some of the plain hand-made pottery found in post-Roman levels may well have been made by British people rather than by immigrant Anglo-Saxons. As masonry buildings in both town and countryside crumbled, they were sometimes replaced by timber structures. Such buildings are gradually being recognised in excavations, most notably at Wroxeter. But considerably more archaeological evidence is needed before we can begin to build up a detailed picture of life in Britain in the years following the collapse of Roman rule.

Roman Britain had been divided into a number of districts or cantons which reflected the old pre-Roman tribal areas. These cantons were each administered by a council, drawn from the local landowners, based on the main town in each district. It was presumably these

Fig. 24

councils which, on the breakdown of central control, took over responsibility for their areas. Documentary sources suggest that, in some areas at least, corporate responsibility was replaced by a monarchical system, where control was exercised by local 'tyrants'.

The date and nature of the earliest Anglo-Saxon settlement is one of the most controversial topics of Early Anglo-Saxon studies. Traditionally according to documentary sources, the Anglo-Saxon settlement began in the mid-fifth century, with the movement of peoples from North-west Europe, according to Bede, the Angles, Saxons and Jutes of modern north-west Germany and Denmark. However, some scholars have argued that the earliest settlements began in the fourth century when groups of Germanic mercenaries and their families were brought to Britain under treaty and given land, in exchange for which they were expected to assist in the defence of Britain against barbarian attacks. Certain types of pottery and metalwork, particularly belt-fittings, have been cited as evidence for this. Other archaeologists however see some at least of these belt-fittings as part of the uniform of auxiliary troops stationed in Britain as sections of the Roman army. Some of these troops may have remained in Britain after the withdrawal of the main army.

The story of two Germanic leaders, Hengist and Horsa, who were invited by one of the British leaders, perhaps Vortigern, in the first half of the fifth century to settle in South-east Britain in exchange for military services, is well-known. It has led some archaeologists to suggest that the first stage of the fifth century Anglo-Saxon settlement was planned and some of the British leaders settled groups of peoples from North-west Europe in certain areas to help protect a district.

There is evidence from the area of the East Anglian Kingdom (the modern counties of Norfolk and Suffolk, and Cambridgeshire east of Newmarket and Ely) for settlement here during the first phase of Anglo-Saxon immigration. There is a growing corpus of archaeological objects which can be closely matched with finds along the North Sea coast of Denmark, Germany and Holland and dated to the period *c.* 410–470. Such items include barred bone combs with zoomorphic projections, certain types of hand-made pottery including carinated bowls and a number of brooch types, for example very simple cruciform brooches, supporting-arm and simple equal-arm brooches and certain types of disc brooches. These have been found in Norfolk and the extreme north of Suffolk, that is, from the area of the old Roman Icenian canton administered from the town of *Venta Icenorum* at

Caistor St. Edmund. Even within this part of the region they are largely absent from the core area of late Roman population and wealth along the eastern edge of the Fens. The majority of Roman villa estates are found in this area and it seems likely that during much of the fifth century at least the land here remained in British ownership and that these landowners were able to exclude the new settlers from their lands. It is likely that British farmers continued to cultivate their lands in other parts of Norfolk and north Suffolk and that they lived and worked alongside the new settlers. It is possible too that the rest of Suffolk or much of it remained under British control. The possibility however that this part of Suffolk became largely depopulated cannot be ignored. The old theory that the Anglo-Saxon settlers seized their land at the point of the sword, slaying or enslaving those British farmers who did not escape to a new life in the fastnesses of western Britain can no longer be upheld at least in East Anglia, although it is likely that some land was fought over. It is impossible from archaeological evidence to determine if British rulers invited Germanic mercenaries to Britain and gave them land or if there were groups of Britons who were sufficiently powerful to prevent new immigrants who landed uninvited in East Anglia from settling in certain areas.

It is difficult too to say at what point within the period *c.* 410–470 the first settlers came to this region. As has been said, the archaeological evidence is derived mainly from stray finds and from cemeteries. The number of records of Anglo-Saxon metal objects has increased enormously since the advent of the metal-detector, but the majority of such finds clearly lack any context. The cemeteries of this period only contain cremation burials. The bodies were burnt, usually fully dressed, and the bones collected and placed in hand-made pots. Many of the grave-goods found in these urns are thus damaged by fire and it is impossible to determine if they were heirlooms or newly-made. It was in this period that the cemeteries at Caistor St. Edmund, Spong Hill in North Elmham and Castle Acre in Norfolk and at Lackford and Eye in Suffolk, and probably others, began. It is difficult too to be certain how far the distribution of cemeteries reflects the distribution of settlements. Dr. Hills has suggested that the Spong Hill cemetery which contained over two thousand cremation burials and some sixty inhumation burials was used by more than one settlement.

Very few settlement sites of the period have been recognised and fewer still excavated. We are fortunate however that one of the most thoroughly investigated settlements of the Early Anglo-Saxon period in Britain is found in East Anglia and began in this first phase.

This site, at West Stow, is on a small knoll beside the Lark in the Breckland of North-west Suffolk. Pottery and metalwork found here show that the settlement had become established by *c.* 450. It was never occupied by more than three or four family groups. Each family had a rectangular timber hall, some 33 feet to 39 feet (10 to 12m) long, and with a central hearth, around which lay a number of other, much smaller buildings. These latter buildings belong to a common type associated with the Anglo-Saxons in Britain and on the continent. Each consists of a rectangular pit, about 13 feet (4m) long, with one, three or four post-holes at either end. Traditionally these were thought to be pit-dwellings in which people lived in conditions of great squalor. But at West Stow there was clear evidence that these pits had been covered with a wooden floor and that the building had vertical wooden walls. Some of them had internal hearths, the wooden floor being protected by clay, and were presumably used to live in, others were used for storage or as workshops, for instance as weaving sheds.

The villagers lived by farming and were largely self-sufficient. They grew grain—wheat, barley, oats and rye— and perhaps other crops in the fields beside the village. They kept sheep, goats, cattle, pigs, hens and geese, cats and dogs. The wool was spun and woven into cloth for their own use and perhaps for sale. Animal bones and deer antlers were worked into a variety of objects, including combs. There is evidence for smithing iron, and pottery making, and they must have worked wood though little evidence remains.

It is dangerous to generalise from a single site, but it is likely that most, if not all, of the Anglo-Saxon settlers of the initial phase must have lived by this simple peasant style of farming.

There is little evidence at West Stow for any real change in life style and of the economy of the settlement in the period *c.* 470–570. But the distribution of stray finds and cemeteries suggest that there was a considerable expansion of Anglo-Saxon settlement in this second phase.

The cemeteries established in the mid-fifth century continued in use but the number increased dramatically and the distribution became more widespread; the main concentration is still found in Norfolk and north Suffolk, although a number have been found in South-east Suffolk, particularly in the area of the rivers Deben and Orwell. Inhumation became a common burial rite. Sometimes such burials are found in association with, and contemporary with, cremation burials. In other cemeteries inhumation is the predominant, or even exclusive, rite. Some of the burials were beneath barrows; such structures have been identified at Spong Hill, Pensthorpe and Morning Thorpe in Norfolk.

Grave-goods continued to be placed in many graves and much of the pottery and metalwork is of insular Anglo-Saxon style. A careful study of the details and styles of decoration, particularly of pottery, has shown that local workshops were developing in this period though it is uncertain if the products were traded out over a limited area from a single workshop or if the craftsmen travelled around a number of communities producing pots within the settlements they visited.

Direct parallels with continental material, such as were clearly apparent in the earlier phase of settlement, are only very occasionally found. But a number of types of metalwork show cultural links with Scandinavia and it is apparently from there that a new dress accessory, the wrist-clasp, comes. These fasteners, essentially a decorative hook and eye, were used at the cuff of women's sleeves in Anglian areas of Britain. Large numbers have recently been recovered from the cemetery at Morning Thorpe in Norfolk.

The increase in the number of cemeteries, the introduction of burial by inhumation, and new dress accessories, suggest the immigration of new settlers from the continent, perhaps from the traditional homelands of the first phase settlers or perhaps, as John Hines has recently suggested, from Norway. But this increase in population may be apparent rather than real and may be the result of the assimilation of the Anglo-Saxon culture by the native population. Or, of course, as a result of both factors.

The nature and quality of some of the grave-goods in these cemeteries and certain burial practices suggest that social stratification was beginning to develop within Anglo-Saxon society. Two of the male graves excavated in the Spong Hill cemetery were clearly special. In both, deep burial pits had been lined with timber to form wooden chambers which were covered with a barrow. Rich grave goods might have been expected from such graves, but unfortunately one at least had been robbed.

The end of this phase saw the emergence of the East Anglian dynasty, the Wuffingas or followers of Wuffa. Historical sources indicate that Wehha became the first king *c.* 550–60 and that he was succeeded about 570 by his son Wuffa.

It is clear that after 570 there were both cultural and social changes. Many of the brooch types characteristic of the second phase disappear, suggesting a change in female dress. By now burial is predominantly by inhumation but some cremations date from this period. Social stratification seems to have increased if one compares, for instance, the burials excavated at Thornham in north Norfolk, many of which were accompanied only by a bronze buckle and an iron knife with those found at Sutton Hoo, Pakefield and Ixworth in Suffolk.

In 1856 a grave was discovered at Ixworth which contained the iron fittings of a bed, a gold and garnet cross and the face-plate of a gold and garnet disc-brooch. Part of a similar brooch and a plain gold pendant were found in 1982 at Bloodmoor Hill, Pakefield, just south of Lowestoft. Here, in 1758, were found in a barrow an onyx intaglio, a gold Visigothic coin, a garnet necklace and perhaps a crystal engraved with a cross. Such burials demonstrate that others beside the royal house could afford rich and exotic objects. We must consider here too Snape, the site of the only other certain Anglo-Saxon ship burial apart from Sutton Hoo. In 1862 nine or ten barrows stood on the heath; five or six of these were large, that is, up to 72 feet (22m) in diameter and over 5 feet (1.5m) high. Excavations revealed that one mound contained a boat, about 48 feet (14m) long, which contained a gold ring, parts of two glass vessels, 'jasper', and some 'dirty red human hair' wrapped in cloth. The burial had been robbed. Only the gold ring, and one of the glass vessels survive. The best parallel to the gold ring, set with a late antique onyx intaglio, is that from grave 1732 at Krefeld-Gellep which was buried *c.* 530–40. A similar mid-sixth century date is suggested for the surviving claw beaker. Both could have been old when buried but it seems possible that the Snape burial is earlier than the boat burials so far investigated at Sutton Hoo. The remains of a large number of cremation urns have been recovered from the site, from the area around the mounds and from the make-up of some of the mounds themselves. These range in date from the fifth to perhaps the seventh century. Unfortunately the status of the person buried at Snape cannot be determined, but clearly he was of high rank.

The burial in mound 1 at Sutton Hoo is therefore the richest of a number of burials found in the kingdom which provide evidence for a wealthy elite as suggested by Bede. Rich burials of the later sixth and early seventh century have been found elsewhere in Britain. Some were inhumations in barrows, others, such as Asthall in Oxfordshire, were cremations. Unfortunately all are old finds, imperfectly recorded. But enough survives both in the surviving objects and in the records to show that most aspects of the great Sutton Hoo burial were not unique, it is the quantity and quality of the objects recovered that make it pre-eminent. The inhumation burials found at Broomfield in Essex and Taplow in Buckinghamshire in particular can be compared with Sutton Hoo. Both were men's burials. Both contained the traditional wealthy man's armoury of shield, spears and sword, the sword from Broomfield being accompanied by a gold pyramid set with garnets. The men wore gold and garnet jewellery, and the man at Broomfield had been buried in a cloak with embroidered edges using gold wire. Many other textiles were recovered from this burial. Drinking horns, glass vessels, buckets and bronze vessels had been placed in these burials. Broomfield also contained wooden cups with bronze rims, an iron cauldron and a lamp similar to that from Sutton Hoo. Taplow contained a Coptic bowl, bone draughtsmen and a lyre. It is the absence of symbols of authority such as the great whetstone and regalia which sets the great ship-burial at Sutton Hoo apart.

The gradual change in the settlement pattern from small groups of farmsteads held by a single family or kin group such as that excavated at West Stow to large estates, each with a controlling centre, perhaps began at this time. Rendlesham, Butley and Barham, all in south-east Suffolk, are possible centres for such estates. By the mid-seventh century, in certain parts of the region at least, the settlement pattern seems to have changed, but that is beyond the scope of this survey.

Postscript

Some readers may be surprised by the omission of place-name evidence for determining the pattern of settlement and of reference to the most impressive field monuments of the Early Anglo-Saxon period. These latter are the linear earthworks, the long banks and ditches found in the western part of the region. These dykes vary in length and size. Most cut across lines of Roman roads and each ends in a natural barrier such as marshland, a river or in forest. The most impressive is the Devil's Dyke which runs for over seven miles from the Fens at Reach in Cambridgeshire, over Newmarket Heath to a former forest at Wood Ditton. This huge earthwork seems to form the boundary with East Anglia.

The date and function of these earthworks is uncertain. The Fossditch of south-west Norfolk was constructed after *c.* 390 and it is thought that all are of post-Roman date. Some archaeologists have seen these earthworks as defences or boundaries thrown up by the indigenous British population between them and the Anglo-Saxon settlers, suggesting a fifth-century date. Others have seen them as political boundaries connected with the expansion of the East Anglian kingdom in the seventh century, or as an East Anglian response to a Mercian threat later in that century. It may well be that they are not all contemporary nor constructed for the same purpose.

When the first edition of this book was written it was still generally accepted that the areas of earliest Anglo-Saxon settlement in parts of England could be identified by place-names with the suffix *-ingas* added to a man's name, for instance Snoring in Norfolk and Gipping in Suffolk. The settlements of the second stage were thought to be those with the suffix *-ingaham*, such as Felmingham (Norfolk) or Heveningham (Suffolk). It had been realised for many years that there was little close coincidence between these place-names and the archaeological evidence, in particular the pagan cemeteries which began in the fifth century. A series of studies begun in the 1960s by place-name specialists suggest that settlements ending in -*ham* (a village), found in some parts of England, are among the earliest Anglo-Saxon settlements; but there are difficulties in separating these from place-names with the suffix -*hamm*. In 1973 Barrie Cox published a study of the early place-names of the East Midlands and East Anglia. He concluded that here the -*ham* names were settlements likely to have been established in the fifth–sixth centuries. His distribution map shows them clustering around the lines of Roman roads. Other studies have shown that certain topographic names are likely to have a very early origin. Before real use can be made of this evidence there is a need for extensive archaeological survey and excavation and close co-operation between archaeologists and place-name specialists in interpreting the results.

BIBLIOGRAPHICAL SUMMARY

S INCE THE publication of the first edition of my father's book many books and papers on Sutton Hoo have appeared. Many of them are included in the bibliographies in the books listed below. A few of the many new books on the Early Anglo-Saxon period are noted at the beginning of this summary. These have good bibliographies.

Arnold, C.J. 1984 *Roman Britain to Saxon England*

Bruce-Mitford, R.L.S., 1974 *Aspects of Anglo-Saxon Archaeology: Sutton Hoo and Other Discoveries*

Bruce-Mitford, R.L.S., et al, 1975–1983 *The Sutton Hoo Ship-Burial* vols. 1, 2, 3 (pts I & II)

Carey-Evans, A., 1986 *The Sutton Hoo Ship-Burial*

Gelling, M., 1978 *Signposts to the Past* (an up-to-date survey of place-name evidence)

Myres, J.N.L., 1986 *The English Settlements*

Rahtz, P., Dickinson, T. and Watts, L., 1980 *Anglo-Saxon cemeteries 1979* BAR British Series 2

West, S.E., 1985 *West Stow, The Anglo-Saxon Village* East Anglian Archaeology Report No 24

Several East Anglian Anglo-Saxon cemeteries have been or soon will be, published in *East Anglian Archaeology*. (Details from the Centre of East Anglian Studies, University of East Anglia, Norwich NR4 7TJ).

B.G.

To provide a full scholar's bibliography here is unnecessary. So much of the relevant matter is published in articles in learned journals that it would be fulsome to name them all. However, the main papers dealing with the Sutton Hoo find are first listed and in these full bibliographical references may be found. I have then made a selection of the more important works in English, in which further references occur, and for the boats I have added a few references to publications in other languages where this seemed desirable.

The first account of the excavation is by C. W. Phillips, 'The Excavation of the Sutton Hoo Ship-Burial', in *Antiquaries Journal*, 20 (1940) and a description of the ship by him is also given in 'The Sutton Hoo Burial Ship', *Mariner's Mirror*, 26 (1940). Constructive criticism of this by R. C. Anderson appears in Vol. 28 (1942) of the same publication; this volume also contains Guy Maynard's 'The Smaller Boat from Sutton Hoo'. A more general account by Mr. Phillips, 'The Excavation of the Sutton Hoo Ship Burial', is in *Recent Archaeological Excavations in Britain* (edited R. L. S. Bruce-Mitford, London 1956).

In 1940, the editor of *Antiquity* devoted the March number of Vol. 14 to Sutton Hoo and its treasures. The contents include: 'I. The Excavation', by C. W. Phillips; 'II. The Gold Ornaments', 'III. The Large Hanging-bowl', 'IV. The Archaeology of the Jewellery', all by T. D. Kendrick; 'V. The Silver', by Ernst Kitzinger; 'VI. The Coins: A Summary', by O. G. S. Crawford; 'VII. The Salvaging of the Finds', by W. F. Grimes and 'VIII. Who was he?' by H. Munro Chadwick. Other preliminary descriptive articles appeared in the *British Museum Quarterly*, 13 (1939) and notes by T. D. Kendrick on a Celtic masked whetstone and the Sutton Hoo gourd-cups appeared in *Antiquaries Journal*, 21 (1941).

Since the war, important papers have been published by R. L. S. Bruce-Mitford. They include *The Sutton Hoo Ship Burial*: A Provisional Guide (London: British Museum, 1947), 'Saxon Rendlesham', *Proceedings of the Suffolk Institute of Archaeology* 24 (1948) and in the following year (1949) in the same publication, Vol. 25, appeared his 'The Sutton Hoo Ship-Burial', a long paper of prime importance. Here also may be mentioned his 'The Snape Boat-grave', in Vol 26 (1952) of the same *Proceedings*. This paper gives full references to the original descriptions by Davidson, Hele and Francis. Other papers by Mr. Bruce-Mitford include 'The Sutton Hoo musical instrument' *Archaeological News Letter*, 1 (1949), 'The Problem of the Sutton Hoo Cenotaph'. *Archaeological News Letter*, 2 (1950) which summarises a lecture and 'The Sutton Hoo Ship-burial' which appears in an appendix in R. H. Hodgkin's *A History of the Anglo-Saxons* (Third edition, Oxford 1952). This book is itself a valuable general history of our period and need not be mentioned again. Professor Sune Lindqvist's important paper, 'Sutton Hoo and Beowulf', translated from the Swedish, is in *Antiquity*, 22 (1948). H. Maryon's papers, 'The Sutton Hoo Shield' and 'The Sutton Hoo Helmet', appeared in *Antiquity*, 20 (1946) and 21 (1947) respectively.

An attempt by Dr. Gordon Ward to maintain the attribution of the cenotaph to Raedwald appeared as 'The Silver Spoons from Sutton Hoo', in *Antiquity*, 26 (1952). This was answered by Mr. Bruce-Mitford later in the same volume and his paper, 'Sutton Hoo: A Rejoinder' was followed immediately by P. H. Grierson's 'The Dating of the Sutton Hoo Coins'. Other interesting papers are J. W. Walker's 'The battle of Winwaed and the Sutton Hoo ship burial', in *Yorkshire Archaeological Journal*, part 145 (1948) and Sir Frank Stenton's 'The East Anglian Kings of the Seventh Century', in *The Anglo-Saxons* (edited by P. Clemoes, London, 1959). Miss V. I. Evison's 'Early Anglo-Saxon Inlaid Metalwork', in *Antiquaries Journal*, 35 (1955) is also of interest.

A 'Chronological Bibliography' of writings dealing with Sutton Hoo was published by F. P. Magoun in *Speculum*, Vol. xxix (1954) and this J. B. Bessinger supplemented in the same journal for 1958. The standard history of the Anglo-Saxon period is Sir Frank Stenton's *Anglo-Saxon England* (Second edition, Oxford, 1947) and D. M. Wilson has also published a general survey of Anglo-Saxon archaeology in his *The Anglo-Saxons* (London, 1960), in which he discusses some of the Sutton Hoo problems. A more specialized book, H. R. Ellis Davidson's *The Sword in Anglo-Saxon England*, (Oxford, 1962) discusses 'ring-swords' and illustrates many examples. Pattern-welding is also described and illustrated.

The standard editions of the early chroniclers in Latin or Anglo-Saxon are well-known to students and need not be enumerated. For English renderings, a translation of the manuscripts collectively known as *The Anglo-Saxon Chronicle* (translated by G. N. Garmonsway) has been published (1953) by J. M. Dent & Sons in the Everyman Library. This Library also contains a translation of Bede's *Ecclesiastical History of the English Nation* (1910) and Professor R. K. Gordon's *Anglo-Saxon Poetry* (revised edition 1954). The latter, which includes 'Beowulf', is rendered in English prose and is a valuable anthology of the early work. Gildas' *De Excidio Six Old English Chronicles* (edited by J. A Giles) in Bohn's nineteenth-century 'Antiquarian Library', now not easily obtained. Translations of *Beowulf* and Bede's *History* have also been published by Penguin Books Ltd.

The writings of Edward Thurlow Leeds are far too numerous to be listed here. His important books are *The Archaeology of the Anglo-Saxon Settlements* (Oxford, 1913), *Celtic Ornament in the British Isles down to A.D. 700* (Oxford, 1933) in which he deals with the problem of the hanging-bowls, *Early Anglo-Saxon Art and Archaeology* (Oxford, 1936) and *A Corpus of Early Anglo-Saxon Great Square-headed Brooches* (Oxford, 1949). Of his many papers, 'The Distribution of the Anglo-Saxon Saucer Brooch . . .', *Archaeologia* 63 (1912), 'The Early Saxon Penetration of the Upper Thames area', *Antiquaries Journal*, 13 (1933), 'The Distribution of Angles and Saxons archaeologically considered', *Archaeologia*, 91 (1945) and 'Denmark and Early England', *Antiquaries Journal*, 26 (1946), are perhaps the most important. A full list of his works was published in his *Festschrift* volume, *Dark-Age Britain* (edited by D. B. Harden, London, 1956). This valuable book comprises many papers; those referred to in the text of this book include 'Romano-Saxon Pottery', by J. N. L. Myres, 'Irish Enamels . . .', by Françoise Henry, 'The Jutes of Kent', by C. F. C. Hawkes, 'The Anglo-Saxon Settlement in Eastern England', by T. C. Lethbridge and 'Glass Vessels . . .', by D. B. Harden.

Reginald Smith's important surveys are to be found in the relevant volumes of the Victoria County Histories in which, county by county, he described the 'Anglo-Saxon Remains'. His also was the British Museum *Guide to Anglo-Saxon and Foreign Teutonic Antiquities* (1923), now alas out of print. His other very numerous papers are scattered through the publications of the Society of Antiquaries of London. Professor G. Baldwin Brown's best work is in the various volumes of his *The Arts in Early England*, the first of which was published in 1903. Those dealing with finds from the graves are volumes 3 and 4, 'Saxon Art and Industry in the Pagan Period' (London, 1915). His *Arts and Crafts of our Teutonic Forefathers* (London, 1910) may also be used with profit. Sir Thomas Kendrick's studies of Anglo-Saxon art are spread through many papers; their substance, with his considered views, are expounded in his *Anglo-Saxon Art to A.D. 900* (London, 1938). Of the papers, three must be mentioned here, 'British Hanging-bowls', *Antiquity*, 6 (1932), 'Polychrome Jewellery in Kent', *Antiquity*, 7 (1933) and 'St. Cuthbert's Pectoral Cross and the Wilton and Ixworth Crosses', in *Antiquaries Journal*, 17 (1937). R. F. Jessup's *Anglo-Saxon Jewellery* (London, 1950) may also be conveniently mentioned here. Another important book, Nils Åberg's *The Anglo-Saxons in England during the early centuries after the invasion* (Uppsala and Cambridge, 1926), is mainly devoted to an exhaustive survey of all the known examples of cruciform and other brooches and the establishment of a detailed chronology based on their development.

Of cemeteries in our East Anglian area an excellent survey to 1938 may be found in Rainbird Clarke's 'Norfolk in the Dark Ages, A.D. 400–800', in *Norfolk Archaeology*, 27 (1938 and 1939), which also includes 'The Anglo-Saxon Pottery of Norfolk', by J. N. L. Myres. There is no detailed survey of Suffolk material later than that of Reginald Smith in the *Victoria County History* (Vol. I, London, 1911), but Mr. Clarke's *East Anglia* (1960) summarises the remains from the two counties in Chapter VIII. For that part of Cambridgeshire included in our area, T. C. Lethbridge's survey of 'Anglo-Saxon Cambridgeshire' in the *Victoria County History* (Vol. 1, London, 1938) is the most relevant. But mention must be made of a famous pioneer work, Sir Cyril Fox's *The Archaeology of the Cambridge Region* (Cambridge, 1923), still an essential source book on which all later work has been based. The Ipswich cemetery was described by N. F. Layard in 'An Anglo-Saxon Cemetery in Ipswich', *Archaeologia*, 60 (1907). Mr. Lethbridge has published reports on his excavations in several cemeteries near the Cambridgeshire-Suffolk border in both the *Proceedings* and the *Quarto Publications* of the Cambridge Antiquarian Society. Some East Anglian remains may be found pictured in colour in J. Y. Akerman's *Remains of Pagan Saxondom* (London, 1855) and the finds from the Little Wilbraham cemetery are described and illustrated in colour in the Hon. R. C. Neville's *Saxon Obsequies* . . . (London, 1852). *The Mildenhall Treasure* (Second edition, London: British Museum, 1955) is a beautifully-illustrated handbook to this important hoard, written by J. W. Brailsford. The Broomfield grave, first described by Sir Hercules Read in the *Proceeding of the Society of Antiquaries* (second series) 15 (1894) is further discussed and illustrated by Reginald Smith in the *Victoria History of the County of Essex* (Vol. 1, Westminster, 1903), where the Forest Gate jewel is also illustrated in colour. The Benty Grange finds were first described by Thomas Bateman in *Ten Years Digging* . . . (London and Derby, 1861). The Hough-on-the-Hill whetstone appears in 'Archaeological Notes for 1956' by D. F. Petch in the *Lincolnshire Architectural and Archaeological Society's Reports and Papers*, 7 (1957).

Dr J. N. L. Myres' descriptions of Anglo-Saxon pagan pottery are in many scattered papers of which 'Some English Parallels to the

Anglo-Saxon Pottery of Holland and Belgium in the Migration Period', *L'Antiquité Classique*, 17 (1948) has special reference to a theme developed in this book. His initial paper on Romano-Saxon pottery has already been mentioned, but this should now be supplemented by the shorter 'Anglo-Saxon Pottery of the Pagan Period', in *Medieval Archaeology*, 3 (1959). In the same volume is J. G. Hurst's supplement to his earlier paper written jointly with S. E. West, 'An Account of Middle Saxon Ipswich Ware' in the 'Proceedings of the Cambridge Antiquarian Society, 50 (1957). For some of the more general historical conclusions, Dr Myres' 'The Adventus Saxonum' in *Aspects of Archaeology* (edited by W. F. Grimes, London, 1951) should be consulted.

A very readable book by Jessie Mothersole, *The Saxon Shore* (London, 1924) may still be read with profit, but since its publication our knowledge has greatly increased and many of its conclusions need to be amended. A book by Donald A. White, *Litus Saxonicum: The British Saxon Shore in Scholarship and History* (Madison, Wisconsin, U.S.A., 1961) is of great interest and has a valuable bibliography, but some of its conclusions are not in accordance with the most recent excavation-evidence. For the general history of the late Romano-British period, R. G. Collingwood and J. N. L. Myres in *Roman Britain and the English Settlements* (Second edition, Oxford, 1937) is still the best, though now outdated.

The published accounts of the early ships are not all easily available as many of them are in German and Scandinavian publications; of some of the English boats there is only the scantiest information. The Walthamstow boat No. 1 is briefly described by W. Robinson in his *History and Antiquities of Hackney in the County of Middlesex* (London, 1842). Walthamstow No. 2 is mentioned by T. V. Holmes in his 'Geological Notes on the New Reservoirs . . .' in *The Essex Naturalist*, 12 (1902) and by A. R. Hatley in *Footnotes to Local History* (Walthamstow, 1932). The finds from this boat-burial are briefly recorded by Dr R. E. M. (now Sir Mortimer) Wheeler in his *London and the Vikings* (London Museum Catalogue, 1927). The few available details of the Yarmouth ship are given by the writer and J. N. Hutchinson in 'Part III. The Archaeological Evidence', in *The Making of the Broads*, by J. M. Lambert *et al.* (London, 1960). The description of the Ashby ship appeared in the *Yarmouth Mercury*, January 8, 1927 and all the available data have been incorporated in this book. The Snape boat and those from Sutton Hoo have already been mentioned.

The Bruges boat found in 1899 and described by E. Jonckheere in

L'origine de la côte de Flandre et le Bateau de Bruges (Bruges, 1903), appears to be later than the Migration Period and so is not described in the survey in Chapter III. Its few preserved remains in the Gruuthuuse Museum were in 1962 in poor condition and little further evidence could be gained from them. Of the Utrecht boat there is a thirty-page account by Hr. Van der Wijk in the *Jaarboekje van 'Oud-Utrecht'* (1932). The later Viking ships, including the Kvalsund and other earlier boats, receive a general description by A. W. Brøgger and H. Shetelig in *The Viking Ships* (London, 1954), a revised English version of their first edition (1951) in Norwegian, the English version being fuller and more satisfactory. An excellent short account in English of the Westfold ships is given by Thorleif Sjøvold in *The Oseberg Find and the other Viking Ship Finds*, a handbook published by the Oslo University Museum (1957). Full details of the Hjortspring boat are available in Danish in *Hjortspringfundet* (Copenhagen, 1937) by G. Rosenberg, K. Jessen and F. Johannessen and of the Halsnøy boat in Norwegian by H. Shetelig in *Bergens Museums Aarbog* (Bergen, 1903). An early account of the Nydam ship, an English version of the finder's original book in Danish, is Conrad Engelhardt's *Denmark in the Early Iron Age* (London, 1866). A full modern description is in German as 'Das Nydamschiff' in *Acta Archaeologica*, I (Copenhagen, 1930) by H. Shetelig. A more satisfactory reconstruction of the steering-mechanism of the Nydam ship is given by J. W. van Nouhuys in 'Some Doubtful Points with regard to the Nydam Ship', in *Mariner's Mirror*, 22 (1936); Shetelig's reconstruction is also criticised by Carl V. Sølver in 'The Rebaek Rudder', in *Mariner's Mirror*, 32 (1946). Engelhardt's other finds from the Danish mosses were described in Danish in *Thorsbjerg Mosefunde* (1863), *Kragehul Mosefunde* (1867) and *Vimose Fundet* (1869), but a short description by H. Jankuhn of the *Nydam und Thorsberg Moorfunde der Eisenzeit* was published by the Schleswig-Holsteinisches Museum (1950) in German. Finally, the Galtabäck ship is described in Swedish by N. Niklasson and Fr. Johannessen in *Galtabäcksbåten och dess Restaurering* (Goteborg, 1933) and further by P. Humbla and L. von Post in *Galtabäcksbåten och tidigt båtbyggen in Norden* (Goteborg, 1937). Its lines are reproduced by Mr. Phillips in *Antiquaries Journal*, 20 (1940).

The Romano-British population was discussed by R. G. Collingwood in 'Town and Country in Roman Britain', *Antiquity*, 3 (1929); H. J. Randall replied with 'Population and Agriculture in Roman Britain', in *Antiquity*, 4 (1930), followed in the same number by Sir Mortimer Wheeler with 'Mr. Collingwood and Mr. Randall'. Dr O. K. Schram's place-name evidence appeared in 'Place-names' in *Norwich and its Region* (Norwich, 1961), the local handbook of the British Association for the Advancement of Science. For the extinct beaver and aurochs, convenient references may be found in J. E. Harting's *British Animals Extinct within Historic Times* (London, 1880), Sir E. Ray Lankester's *Extinct Animals* (London, 1906) and Colin Matheson's *Changes in the Fauna of Wales within Historic Times* (Cardiff: National Museum of Wales, 1932).

The continental literature dealing with the Migration Period is of enormous volume, but a few books and papers may be suggested to outline the continental background. H. M. Chadwick's *The Origin of the English Nation* (Cambridge, 1907), though some of its conclusions must now be modified, is an excellent starting point; H. Shetelig and H. Falk have made a valuable survey in their *Scandinavian Archaeology* (Oxford, 1937). The Vendel graves, so important to Sutton Hoo students, were first described in Swedish (1912) by H. Stolpe and T. J. Arne, but a later edition in French, *La Nécropole de Vendel* (Stockholm, 1927) makes their work more easily accessible to English readers. Two short but valuable surveys by leading German scholars. 'The Continental Home of the English', by H. Jankuhn and 'The Continental Background', by F. Tischler, appeared in *Antiquity*, 26 (1952) and *Medieval Archaeology*, 3 (1959) respectively.

Finally, for the discussions of *Beowulf*, reference should first be made to Professor R. W. Chambers' *Beowulf: An Introduction to the Study of the Poem with a Discussion of the Stories of Offa and Finn* (Second revised edition, Cambridge, 1932). This book has an exhaustive bibliography complete to the time of publication and it need only be supplemented by reference to Professor F. Klaeber's *Beowulf with the Fight at Finnsburg* (Third revised edition, Boston, U.S.A., 1936), Professor D. Whitelock's *The Audience of Beowulf* (Oxford, 1951) and Mrs. N. K. Chadwick's 'The Monsters and Beowulf' in *The Anglo-Saxons* (edited by P. Clemoes, London, 1959), in which she suggests the possibility of an East Anglian origin for the poem for other reasons than those advanced above. For the 'Ynglingasaga', a convenient edition in English of Snorre Sturlason's *Heimskringla* is in two volumes in the Everyman Library.

Mention may also be made of a paper by Rosemary J. Cramp, 'Beowulf and Archaeaology', in *Medieval Archaeology*, Vol. I (1957) and Professor C. L. Wrenn's 'Sutton Hoo and Beowulf' in *Mélanges de Linguistique et de Philologie* (Paris, 1959) which also gives the *Beowulf* poem an East Anglian origin.

INDEX